ARNA

THE JOURNAL OF THE UNIVERSITY OF SYDNEY ARTS STUDENT SOCIETY

2011

First published 2011 by Darlington Press
Funded by The University of Sydney Union and The University of Sydney
Faculty of Arts

ISBN: 978-1-921364-20-4

Fisher Library F03
University of Sydney
NSW 2006 Australia
Email: sup.info@sydney.edu.au

Cover design by Phoebe Johnson

CREDITS

Editors-in-Chief
Richard Withers
Anne Widjaja

General Editors
Alex McKinnon
Elizabeth Goralewski

Creative Writing Editors
Paul Ellis
Anna Westbrook

Poetry Editors
Bryant Apolonio
Dominic McNeil
Danielle Chiaverini

Critical Editors
Simone Van Nieuwenhuizen
Jonathan Dunk
Isabelle Ho

Copy Editors
Jenny Sun
Gemma Davies
Eloise Callaghan

Designers
Nadia Junaideen
Phoebe Johnson
Robert Colman
Alistair Stevenson

Visual Arts Editors
Feng Guo
Robby Magyar

THANKS TO

The University of Sydney Union
The University of Sydney Faculty of Arts
The Sydney Arts Students Society
Contributors
Jacqui Munro
Agata Mrva-Montoya

CONTENTS

Adam Spencer | FOREWORD

It may seem heretical to some that a graduate of the University of Sydney, in of all things, pure mathematics, would write the introduction to a compilation of work from the University's Arts Society. Well in my defence, my four years of mathematics, replete with complex numbers, group theory and multivariable calculus, was undertaken as part of my Arts degree and as I have always said, 'my Arts degree … was the best nine and a half years of my life'.

Just today in my 'other job', (the breakfast radio show that I perform to pay the bills when penning introductions for student literature almanacs doesn't quite cover my obligations), I was reflecting on a curious anniversary—30 years since the first mobile phone call was made in Australia. A call that was made on a 14-kilo battery-powered behemoth, that could store up to 16 phone numbers and cost a mere $17,000 in today's moolah!

I didn't check, but I presume said call was made by someone pulling in towards Redfern Station, shouting 'you'll have to call me back … I'm a wanker'.

Now strictly my time at University came after that first mobile call was made, but I certainly don't recall seeing any such devices. In a world where *Honi* was laid up in the 'Bromide Room' and people eyed jealously the Union Recorder's mint fresh recently purchased Apple Mac Classic with it's four … count them four!!! megs of memory, the idea of reading 'The Best of ARNA' on one's phone having had it flicked wirelessly through the ether was beyond fanciful.

But despite our hurtling headlong into the digital age, where you can carry in your pocket more memory than they would have spent on 10,000 space shuttles, some things don't change. In 1990, as in 2011, as in the 1850s when students first attended the University of Sydney, as for 40,000 years previous on this beautiful and well-loved continent, the power of words has held sway.

Be they written in the Queens English by the first mass-produced fountain pens of the 1880s, passed on from mother to son softly in Dharug tongue around a beachside fire or txtd in smsish simply 2G2B4G, the power of words to inspire and seduce us remains unchanged.

And so it is here. This journal is full of some great writing. Certainly not perfect, but hey, apart from perhaps the final scene in ***, has there ever been such a thing as written perfection.

Well whether this compile whispers in your ears like sweet sussurance, cascades like a timid tintinnabulation or kicks you so hard in the macula of utricle that you need a good lie down I can only hope that it did indeed make noise for you.

May Creative Arts at Australia's oldest university continue on its noisy way.

Michela Ziady | BABY

'White potato-legs, stodgy flesh
Dumpling knees below powdery bum
Swollen eyes; mellow-marsh cheeks.'
Stop smoking, loose pants, start yoga and chart ovulating hope.

Ultrasounds stealing hidden water fingers
Dad's hands; mum's toes.
Moon circles of life—nudging hello
Moments that murmur, a secret from inside: ours.

Wallpaper of white dandelions behind her speckled rocking chair
New lights from Thailand, the vintage doll
From Granny Gillian and Granddad Frank.
A ready room and empty cot, awaiting baby's small sleep.

Hospital bag. Zip. Midwife's mobile number from fridge
Door. Dad breathing too
Contractions tracked and
Closing, coming, keep going.

Placenta tearing at the uterus. Upside down delirium-pain
Dilations stop. Knot. Induce.
That epidural for life, for air becomes an emergency C-section too.

Late. Fifteen hours of baby. Still. Pulled out blue.

James Watson | **& BELOW THE TABLE**

& below the table, near the shorter leg, was the old AM radio that Daddy had ignored for years. We bought it for him on the same day that Vincent had climbed onto the roof, & fell, & wrecked both his knee & the rainwater draining system, at the same time. At first, Daddy liked the radio, & listened to the radio in the garage, during the hours he spent trying to fix the drain for the roof. But after he finally fixed it, & reinstalled it back into our household, he never turned the damn thing on again. Occasionally he'd say something like 'I'm gonna fix the shorter leg of the table,' & we'd hope he'd turn on that radio when he saw it on his way down to the floor to inspect the table leg, but he'd usually look at it for less than a second, & begin work on that shorter leg, something which he could never fix because he never knew how to begin with extending the leg of a table, so he'd just place some old books that he'd never read under the leg & claim that he'd fixed it, but we knew that it was still the same wonky leg that we used to hold our food, or schoolbooks, or bills, or mortgages, or birth certificates, or death certificates, or anything else we had in our hands that we could no longer hold.

Daddy finally chose to sell the damn AM radio, & he put up signs in the street that said 'AM Radio: Free', & then he wrote our address beneath. We'd thought that somebody'd take the damn thing that very afternoon, but nobody even seemed to take notice until two months later, when a man we'd never seen before (& we'd seen everybody in the town because it is a small town—you know everyone in it, from their name, to their birthday, to their favourite football team, to their secret love affairs, to their not so secret love affairs, to the names of their childhood dogs, to their hidden birthmarks or tattoos), & he had said that he was interested but wanted to know why the radio was free, & wanted to know if there was something wrong with the radio, & Daddy said that there wasn't anything wrong, & he just wanted to get rid of it, & the man (who seemed to limp everywhere but I didn't think he had something wrong with his leg) said that he didn't want to get a radio that was already broken, & left our front yard (which was the place where we were having the conversation).

Daddy adjusted the signs, to make them say AM Radio: $5. Later that afternoon, a man (who wore a very long coat, the kind that nearly reaches one's ankles) came to our front yard & asked Daddy about the radio, & he gave Daddy $5, & Daddy gave him the AM radio, & both parties involved in the exchange were very happy. I asked Daddy if there was some moral, or lesson to be learnt from all this, & he said that he was confused about my question & that I should go onto the roof & fix the rain water drain because it's clogged again.

James Watson | # THE MAN

The Man, if he could, would he, should he consider, think about, wonder, tolerate, undergo, experience, enjoy the feeling, the thought, the pleasure, the warmth, the coolness, the e-z baked comfort of walking, ambling, traversing, running, biking, jumping into the middle of the desert, wasteland, forest, jungle, alienated farm and let his beard, facial hair grow, rise, produce, pop up, thrive, arrive on his face, chin, cheek, upper lip and not lose sleep, rest, catnap, slumber land, sack time, a few Zs over his work, job, occupation, boss, employer and forget about his responsibilities, duties, burdens, obligations, chores, wife, children, brothers, sisters, dead mother and father, uncles, aunts, cousins, second cousins, long-lost cousins, can't-be-lost cousins, forgotten nephews and nieces, forgotten birthdays, anniversaries, weddings, funerals, cremations, christenings, bar mitzvahs, bat mitzvahs, dentist appointments, doctor appointments, funny lumps that you ignore, lunches, dinners, brunches, books to read, songs to hear, films to see, movies that can't be missed, spilt coffee, spilt milk, lumps in tea, no hot water, cold shower, no dry towels, no spare change, no exact change, bumping, crowding, chaos, sound, fury—if the man could, he would run to that wasteland and lie down, stretch his hands above his head, and watch his arms burn in the sun.

Robert Ribbons |

CHEMOTHERAPY

At night
in the white cloisters
of this urban grotto
nurses levitate, casting
spells through saline drips
A morphine metamorphosis

In the dark glass
of the window
My hair is gone

Skin bruised
the crushed texture
Of yellow poppies

Ulcers blister
boil in the pot
Of my throat

Beneath my gown
A monsoon brews
Soon, soon, this body will decay
Singe into ash

My burnt flesh
Carbon paper
A fetid mulch
to feed the gory mouths
Of new begonias

Sam Barnett | # THE IRANIAN.COM

Constructing the national in an era of transnationalism:
Iranian.com as an Iranian virtual community

Given that the internet is a ubiquitous part of life for many people in Iran and the West, there has been relatively little examination of the relationship between the internet and national identities. In Iran, social networks such as Twitter and Facebook have been used to challenge and mobilise against the state. The international media and academia have become interested in the role of Iranian blogs in Iranian reform movements and the 2009 Iranian presidential election protests. However, the focus has primarily been upon the supposed liberating power of the internet in the face of Iran's closed society. There has been far less study of the way that Iranian nationality and nationalism is manifested in online activity. It is therefore both important and interesting to examine online activity in relation to nationalism, precisely because the internet is essentially a stateless world where nationalisms are not contained by state borders. Diasporas are interesting in this respect, as they often have greater access to the internet, as well as more fluid and multifaceted identities. This article will examine just one example of what can be described as a virtual community—the US-based Iranian.com. Looking at the website through the lens of two key thinkers on nationalism, Benedict Anderson and Arjun Appadurai, it becomes evident that the internet can potentially allow Iranians to re-imagine their national community in innovative ways, with a greater focus on individuality and participation in the imagining of the community.

Considering nations beyond the state

Nationalism, as a way of looking at national identity, privileges a particular kind of identity: one that delineates 'the other' by national boundaries. It is an identity which becomes more problematic in cyberspace, yet the very name 'Iranian.com' suggests that the website revolves around the nation as the primary level of identity. There is an important current of modern thought on nationalism that focuses on the socially constructed nature of nations. Perhaps the most systematic discussion of the construction of national consciousness has been from Benedict Anderson, who, writing his seminal text in 1983, viewed nations as 'imagined communities', primarily conceived through representation in the media. Anderson's view is historically situated within Western (especially Protestant) Europe's history of print capitalism, and is connected to the rise of printing in vernaculars, as opposed to Latin. This allowed members of a nation to 'imagine' themselves through printing. Publications were printed in a national language and were distributed widely enough to reach beyond a thin stratum of elite readership.

Building on Anderson's theory, the US-based anthropologist Arjun Appadurai examines the idea of virtual communities and connects the internet to the idea of national identity. While Anderson views nationalism as a historical phenomenon in terms of its development, Appadurai examines nationalism's more modern manifestations. For Appadurai, they 'involve communities of citizens in the territorially defined nation-state who share the collective experience ... of reading books, pamphlets, newspapers, maps and other modern texts together'. This reflects the Andersonian idea of the centrality of print media, but also encompasses modern electronic media. Appadurai's most relevant contribution is not his discussion of nationalism per se, but his ideas about emerging virtual communities. In terms of the form of online communities, Eugenia Siapera suggests a list of six online cultural communicative formats: online discussions; blogs; online poems; prose and pictures, articles; downloads; and dating/marriage sites. Appadurai argues that at the time (1996), virtual communities were limited primarily to facilitating a transnational intelligentsia, and also suggests that the role of these communities is evolving to connect diasporas to their home countries and to each other. Furthermore, he comments on how these virtual communities are able to have direct flows back into spatial communities. As a result, they extend beyond merely being an interesting feature of the internet to being directly relevant to offline nationalisms.

Representing the national in the virtual: Iranian.com

How do Iranian virtual communities renegotiate the relationship between an Iranian homeland and the virtual community? In the past few years Iran has experienced a very rapid increase in internet usage, as have many of the countries with Iranian diaspora communities. For example, the number of internet cafés in Tehran went from only a handful in 2000 to 7000–8000 two years later. This has created unprecedented opportunities for establishing connections between Iranians both inside and outside Iran.

The relevance of blogs

Blogs are one of the most prominent areas of Iranian online expression and connection, and demonstrate a number of similarities to the format of Iranian.com. One of the most important aspects of Iranian blogs is that they provide personal commentary (political, social, literary, etc.) and therefore target specific interest groups. As a result, they have an essentially 'fragmented audience', and generally are not aiming to replace more traditional websites for information and news. Unlike the traditional forms of media, it is not difficult to publish your work on a blog. Online voices are also often anonymous.

Given the high proportion of blogs which are either personal diaries, or topics that cover subjects such as art and information technology, many Iranian blogs do not discuss specifically nationalist subjects. However, some theorists, such as Alexanian (2009), suggest that the use of the internet for Iranians is largely 'mediated by cultural understandings', despite (or perhaps because of) the deterritorialising effect of the internet.

So, if internet use is mediated by cultural understandings, rather than maintaining a connection to the Persian homeland, Persian blogs may serve as a link to an Iranian imagined community grounded in culture, but not territory.

Iranian.com as an Iranian online community: personal and participatory?

Iranian.com (2002) is an interesting example of a diaspora-based Iranian online community. Based in California in the US, the website has been described as a 'scrapbook' by its founder Jahanshah Javid. In essence, the website is compiled from personal articles, as well as visual submissions, about a variety of topics. The personal nature of Iranian.com is a structural factor, but Graham and Khosravi (2002) have also noted a general trend in Iranian online activities towards expressing individuality. Notably, the website has very little agency of its own and is more a network for the connection of the users. As with blogging, it is the personal nature of the articles, as well as the ability of the readers to comment and discuss, that creates the sense of an 'imagined' online community. In some ways, this represents a new participatory approach to conceptualising national communities. The Andersonian idea of the imagined community is strongly grounded in literary studies, especially with regard to the purpose of the newspaper. Yet newspapers are largely non-participatory for readers, so the Andersonian community is not imagined interactively. The informal nature of the material is important because a newspaper, as the traditional Andersonian counterpoint for the imagined community, presents itself as a single official voice of a national narrative. In contrast, Iranian.com presents fragments of many narratives from many different voices.

The range of topics of articles reflects the personal nature of the narratives. While the website has a separate Persian language section, the majority of articles are in English and the site must be navigated in English. The English articles tend to have slightly more politicised topics than that of the Persian articles. The political articles in both languages discuss issues such as regional security in the Middle East, women's rights and democracy. The articles, in keeping with the personal nature of the website, do not necessarily have anything in common. They show the interests of their authors only, rather than the group as a whole. As with blogs, their positions are often quite different and can produce lively debates with other members of the online community. In some cases, the anonymity of the internet gives contributors the freedom to express political views which they otherwise could not or would not share. Graham and Khosravi (2002) make the link between anonymity and the 'threat of persecution', though this is usually less of an issue in diaspora communities. However, the anonymity may still give a greater degree of freedom from social restriction. Additionally, as Siapera notes, internet anonymity often results in a sense of equality for those involved in contributions and discussions.

Iranian.com and outsiders

As an outlet for personal stories, the website is not aiming to promote any sort of national narrative to outsiders (or kharejis, to use the Persian term). However, there is nothing designed to exclude outsiders and being Iranian is not a prerequisite for registration. While Iranian.com does not recount the 'common myths and historical memories' associated with the national community, many of the personal narratives are in fact grounded in these myths and memories. For example, a recent article from user 'siamak vossoughi' discusses his father's writing class in America, which is juxtaposed against the background of the Iranian Revolution, the difficulties of life in a foreign land and being an outsider. Although it is possible to understand the article without any knowledge of Iranian culture or the Iranian-American diaspora, much of the meaning and subtlety derives from common myths and memories.

The ambiguity of 'homeland'

As an online diaspora community, Iranian.com has a certain ambiguity regarding offline territory in both host and home countries. Alexanian sees Iranian.com as representing a distinct link between the offline and online, however, the 'offline' represented by the website is not always clear and fixed. Significantly, only a small percentage of the traffic to Iranian.com comes from Iran, the highest sources of visitors being the United States, Canada, Germany and the United Kingdom.

Certainly the majority of the political articles revolve around Iran as a place, being linked to current events and developments in Iran. In some ways this may serve to 'connect home ... with here', to borrow Collins' phrase, just as a newspaper connects one to the imagined community in Anderson's theory. This is important, because home, or homeland, is a very important idea in nationalist discourse. In a similar vein to Appadurai, R.J. Kaiser (2004) has noted that homelands are not objective facts, but constructs. Therefore, 'nation and homeland ... naturalises [sic] the link between blood and soil', especially as Iranian nationalism has also traditionally had a strong focus on territory and territorial integrity.

Yet the use of English in Iranian.com reflects the way that the online community is ultimately grounded in its offline base in the United States rather than in Iran. The website's photography section presents a degree of Iranian territoriality, such as photos of travels to Iran, but also many albums that reflect the same personal diaspora narratives as the articles, such as user Lida Ghaemi's recent trip to Cambodia or bahmani's photos of Iranians in a recent gay pride parade in Toronto.

One final point that might be worth considering is the renegotiation of identity. In their research on online communities, Siapera (2007), Parker and Song (2007) and Brouwer (2006) have all noted the importance of online communities as sites for discussion and renegotiation of identity (something that is a particular issue with second generation immigrants), rather than expression of fixed or predetermined identities. This is partly structural, with the comments section allowing for direct debate between users. It may also be helpful to think in terms of a singular online 'community' instead of 'communities', as it is often more about reflection and the creation of a sense of community rather than being formal communities. Iranian.com may also act as an environment for members of the Iranian diaspora to come to terms with their homeland(s), where the terms of belonging and citizenship are actively negotiated.

Conclusions

While Iranian.com does not provide a comprehensive picture of Iranian internet usage, it does demonstrate some interesting aspects of re-imagining the nation online. Rather than causing the 'de-imagining' of a national community, the internet allows Iranians in the diaspora and within the country itself to use new technology to re-imagine their nationality and themselves interactively. Perhaps unsurprisingly, Iranian.com does not circumvent the nation, but reaffirms the idea of Iranian identity in the borderless online world. However, it complicates the idea of being Iranian in that the very idea of a grand narrative of history and homeland is rejected (unconsciously perhaps) in favour of localised, individual Iranian narratives. A great deal of the material on Iranian.com is highly politicised, yet it is also personal and segmented, and offers a new, participatory way of imagining the national or diasporic community. While there has been a lot of academic focus on the use of the internet in mobilising against the state, in the case of Iranian.com, the issue of challenging the state is not as significant as challenging the very idea of how 'community' is defined by a single national voice. Instead it facilitates the challenging of ideas about who has the right to narrate and construct this national consciousness.

References

Alexa (2011). Top sites in Iran. [Online]. Available: www.alexa.com/topsites/ countries/IR [Accessed 24 July 2011].

Alexanian JA (2009). Constructing Iran: conflict, community, and the politics of representation in the digital age. PhD Thesis. Irvine, USA: University of California,

——— (2006). Publicly intimate online: Iranian web logs in Southern California. *Comparative Studies of South Asia Africa and the Middle East*, 26(1): 134–45.

Anderson B (2006). *Imagined communities: reflections on the origin and spread of nationalism.* New York: Verso.

Appadurai A (2005). *Modernity at large: cultural dimensions of globalization.* Minneapolis: University of Minnesota Press.

Atabaki T (2005). Introduction: transnationalism and diaspora in Central Asia and the Caucasus. In Atabaki T & Mehendale S (Eds). *Central Asia and the Caucasus: transnationalism and diaspora* (pp. 1–9). Oxon: Routledge.

Brouwer L (2006). Dutch Moroccan websites: a transnational imagery? *Journal of Ethnic and Migration Studies,* 32(7): 1153–68.

Collins FL (2009). Connecting 'home' with 'here': personal homepages in everyday transnational lives. *Journal of Ethnic and Migration Studies,* 35(6): 839–59.

Google (2011). Doubleclick ad planner by Google. [Online]. Available: www.google.com/adplanner/planning/site_profile?hl=en#sit eDetails?identifier=iranian.com&lp=true [Accessed 24 July 2011].

——— Google trends for website: iranian.com. [Online]. Available: trends. google.com/websites?q=Iranian.com&sa=N [Accessed 24 July 2011].

Iranian.com [2010]. Iranian.com: nothing is sacred. [Online]. Available: www.iranian.com [Accessed 24 July 2011].

Kaiser RJ (2004). Homeland making and the territorialization of national identity. In Conversi D (Ed). *Ethnonationalism in the contemporary world: Walker Connor and the study of nationalism.* pp. 229–47. London: Routledge.

Kashani-Sabet F (1999). *Frontier fictions: shaping the Iranian nation, 1804–1946.* Princeton: Princeton University Press.

Khiabany G & Sreberny A (2007). The politics of/in blogging in Iran. *Comparative Studies of South Asia Africa and the Middle East,* 27(3): 563–79.

Khosravi S & Graham M (2002). Reordering public and private in Iranian cyberspace identity, politics, and mobilization. *Identities,* 9(2): 219–46.

Khosronejad P (2011). Some observations on visual representations of the 2009 Iranian presidential election crisis. *Iranian Studies*, 44(3): 395–408.

Mau S (2010). *Social transnationalism: lifeworlds beyond the nation-state*. Oxon: Routledge.

Parker D & Song M (2007). Inclusion, participation and the emergence of British Chinese websites. *Journal of Ethnic and Migration Studies*, 53(7): 1043–61.

Shafee SMM (2003). Globalization and the contradiction between the nation and the state in Iran: the internet case. *Middle East Critique*, 12(2): 189–95.

Siapera E (2007). Multicultural radical democracy and online Islam. In Dahlberg L & Siapera E (Eds.) *Radical democracy and internet: interrogating theory and practice* (pp. 148–67). New York: Palgrave Macmillan.

Smith AD (1991). *National identity*. London: Penguin Books.

Vahabzadeh P (2008). Where will I dwell? A sociology of literary identity within the Iranian diaspora. *Comparative Studies of South Asia Africa and the Middle East*, 28(3): 495–512.

Michael Falk | TUNISIA

'To create a little flower is the labour of ages'—William Black

Winds stir the dust, feet stir the dust, a boy treks to market,
Pounding, pounding, quivering blood in the arteries, pounding
The sinew-fear as a heart that bleeds beats weirder time.

'To create a little flower is the labour of ages,' spoke a prophet,
And this heart of flesh will soon labour in the void,
Infinitely working a wrathful art. In Sidi Bouzid he pounds.

Who can deny him? Robots consume his fruit, food, money,
Deleting data for the Subroutine, little agent of the Network,
But Machinemen cannot atomise his soul.

He speaks—from the desert I come, from the heat that
Time never forgets, from the dirt and water and reality
You cannot process. To the desert I will return.

From the desert I come, with the sands that block
Vision, that corrode the silicon steel manacles,
That fracture your cold. To the desert I will return.

He explodes in the ash. Great clouds swirl in his hair,
His eyes, his fingernails that claw at stones and wood.
He flashes, smites, tears and destroys—Law quails,

Police tremble, Loans shatter, Security knows. Ending
In black chaos Life rears, her red eyes stare at the small,
Burning body of a student alone in that square.

A Crash in the Subroutine—its Robots convulse, circuitry
Shorts from a wave of true data, red force
Sweeping far from the epicentre: Sidi Bouzid, where he pounds.

The Network is torn, Bone-Spiders rattle across the web,
Find their silk is hot embers, where fire
Tears open their System, spreads tweeting and whirring

Along threads that were weaved to repress.
The Network is down, Bone-Spiders rush to TV,
Screening hatred with lies of camaraderie.

But who can deny him? His heart of flesh beats weirder time.
Now Life cradles his body in Death. This part of no part,
This lost one, this dust clod, tight sinew, now burns, screaming—

Love it, my sisters my brothers: there is a Truth in this World!

Bryant Apolonio | # MARGATE SANDS

When June comes, the Sands are doused with wet, and they glisten like the ooze of a wound.

This is the fifth day of the week, first week of the month, and I am walking down Margate Hill. Down the hill—silting the soles of my boots, easing past spinifex and nicker-nut—towards the seashore which I can now hear and taste. I have a blue backpack. I have a metal detector that squeals, trills, whirrs, whimpers arrhythmically, as I pass piles of stones. The machine is deficient. It cannot find non-magnetic alloys, it cannot find materials beyond shallow depth, it cannot find landmines.

'Are you looking for any of those things, Phil?', Lorraine says. She is the only person I know who calls me Phil. Lorraine works at Sands Café, a wooden stall, built a foot-and-a-half above the ground, adorned with tropical affectation: snarling tiki-heads, a plastic hula girl from her boss' dashboard. The smoking area is the only area. A plastic tarpaulin, condensation running down its poreless skin, shelters the three customers who have decided to spend a day by the sea. Lorraine pulls her brown hair back, taut, and ties it into a bun. 'I mean, what kind of metal isn't magnetic?'

My brain says, Copper. My brain says, Aluminium. My brain says, Tungsten; says, Lead. 'Can't think of any!' I reply, smiling, though I am smiling with my teeth. My wrought enthusiasm makes Lorraine uncomfortable, I suppose, because she simply nods and moves to the next table. The other two customers here are a Czech couple, regulars, usually around when I am. The husband seems docile, though I have only spoken to him once. Here are things I have noticed about him:

1. He always spends ten minutes perusing the meal deals, then orders the same pumpkin soup, the same plastic packet of wholemeal crackers.

2. He wears collared shirts with awkward patterns—white blossoms, bats, Santa Clauses in various jovial positions—which he renders damp and dark in the summer time, as he progresses perspiring through his lunch.

3. On his left forearm is a birthmark like a creeping vine.

'You are a strange man, always with your device', he once told me, his observation devoid of malice. He claimed that there were only puddles back where he was born, which half-explained why they were here almost every day.

'The sky is God's dishrag,' I say, when Lorraine returns with a toasted cheese sandwich. Lorraine has plenty of jewellery on her thin wrists, widening into palms, curling into fingers. She sets down my plate. It is warm from resting in the groove of her hand. Her silver bracelets rub together, like whispering leaves. The metal detector would not be able to find those.

'That's clever,' she says. 'It's awful out.'

I take a bite of the sandwich and the tomatoes are hot. I suck in breaths of air to cool them down in my mouth and Lorraine laughs, then stops. Her laughter is like a hiccup. Her eyelashes are as sharp as the prongs of a fork.

'Your eyelashes are beautiful,' I finally say, because this seems like a thing that I'm expected to comment on. I take another bite of my food. Lorraine looks around for any new customers, finds none, pats flour off her linen shirt, then pulls up a chair and sits adjacent to me.

'How long will you be treasure-hunting today, Phil?' she asks.

'I'm looking for interesting things,' I say.

'How long will you be doing that?'

I consider this. 'I'll leave when it's dark.'

'When it's dark,' she repeats. Another question: 'How's your lunch? It's olive bread.'

'It's great olive bread,' I say.

There are exactly five khaki circles on the top slice. I wonder what contribution, and the extent of their contribution, is to the sandwich's flavour (qualities of olives from a jar: briny, acidic, peppery stuffing).

'Today's special,' she says. 'Good luck treasure-hunting.' Lorraine stands up like a churchgoer at the right parts, solemn, automatic. I grip the handle of my metal detector, which is leaning on the edge of the table, when it teeters. Lorraine looks at it, looks at me, then departs, twisting stray hairs between two fingers, rolling silverware into peach-hued napkins.

I finish the sandwich and leave the uneven crusts in the shape of a lightning bolt. As I pay the bill ($6.20), I see languorous smoke rings curl from behind the café. There are boxes there. Ceramic tiles leftover from when there were renovations in the bathroom, last December. One is now used to keep the screen door closed on windy days. My brain forms an image of Lorraine sitting on a box, cross-legged, with her fresh pack of Marlboros, gazing into the dishrag sky above her, tiles clinking like Christmas whenever she shifts her weight.

Today I find fourteen interesting things. In my head I make catalogue of these objects in the order I find them in: 1. a wrench, 2. a locket (green-grey, patinated), 3a. and 3b. safety pins (rusty, unusable), 4. a watch (broken), 5. a glass bottle (sans message), 6a. to 6h. silver coins of varying value and currency. All of these are interesting things.

When I finish in the late afternoon, there is a flock of petrel on the beach. They caw sharply, like children with singed fingers. Leprous strings of seaweed litter the shore around them in weird geometry, beaten black under the sun. Walking over to the birds, I see that there is a man among them throwing handfuls of dusty bread. I approach him.

'No!' the man exclaims. 'You'll frighten them.'

He looks like Jesus. He is Jesus in a frayed parka and salt blue shorts cut at the knee. On his hip is a small nylon pouch. He is barefoot and his toes curl in the sand, fattening the floury surface. When I come nearer he throws bread at me, and the birds inch closer too, testing their bravery. They have the numbers. I ease my way through the excitable flock, like a cyclist in peak hour traffic.

'That's illegal,' I say.

'Blow it out your arse, fascist,' he says, still throwing bread.

He stops when I stand still, his face softening. I set down my machine. 'I subscribe to no law,' he concludes simply. I offer the man my mints, and he replies with a stately nod, taking two.

'If you feed them, they'll forget how to find food for themselves,' I say. His legs are long, bristly with black hairs at the knee.

'But they won't have to find food,' the man says, eating one mint and placing the other in his hip pouch. 'They won't have to find food because I'm always feeding them.' He bites down on the mint, chews it in the back of his mouth. He makes perfect sense! my brain says, which is baffling.

'Hold on,' I say.

'What's that?'

'I said, "hold on".'

He turns his pouch inside out and shakes crumbs onto the sand. 'What should I hold?' In front of us, plateaus float up and vanish as the evening tide swells.

I am worried about these birds. I am worried that this man may not always come to the beach, which is why feeding is illegal. The birds will forget how to find food for themselves. And one day the petrel will come, the gull, the sooty oystercatcher, the wheeling lapwing; they will set down past the swathing shallows, waiting. They will wait with the rigidity of puppets, mute and expectant. They will wait for the bread that was promised. The bread which the LORD hath given them to eat. The bread that always fell unto them from this nylon pouch. They will wait for this man, his sackcloth and his bread, his beaten sandals, his calloused soles, to lead them through the dunes and promontories. But, lo, they will find the

Sands barren, and so too the shrubs behind them, and the asphalt roads, and the nearby café, and there will be few people on the beach, if any, for winter has come.

'That's a lot of responsibility,' I finally croak.

'Responsibility builds character,' he says. He wears a confident smile as I walk away. I can't help but wonder that maybe I'm completely mistaken about the passions and desires of semi-aquatic birds.

The next day is the sixth day of the week, first week of the month, and I'm marching down Margate Hill, in the a.m. cool, with backpack, metal detector, mints, and $6.20 for a toasted cheese sandwich on olive bread.

'Actually the special today is rye,' Lorraine says, when I order.

'Good,' I say. 'I love rye. Bring on the rye.'

'I forgot to put the olive bread in the fridge. It's mouldy.'

'When is your break?'

Underneath the table, my leg is shaking. Underneath the table, I'm tracing random patterns on my knees with my fingertips, like a spell.

'I have lunch at two,' she says.

'Maybe you'd like to walk with me?'

Today I find eleven interesting things, including but not limited to: 1. a pair of reading glasses, wire framed, 2. a set of keys bunched like a fist, 3. their keychain, a plastic skull, 4. the lid of a Parker pen, 5. an elastic hair-tie, pink, 6. a green one, 7. a guitar pick, 8. a twenty dollar note, in my back pocket.

At two o'clock I walk back to the café to get Lorraine. By now, the sky is orange. She walks beside me as I scan the ground. I am scouring with more vigour than I'm accustomed and she is eating a blueberry muffin. I'm nervous but elated. Nervous and elated. Froth lingers at the edges of my boots as the tide retreats (things that resemble sea froth, in the sun: soap, clouds, the emptied contents of a pillow). Lorraine is a kind woman. I feel no pangs of apprehension or urgency when I'm with her. We walk from Sands Café to the craggy rock pool on the other side of the beach. She mostly speaks, and she mostly speaks about herself, but I prefer that. I learn the following things:

1. Lorraine, who I can call Lorrie because we're friends aren't we, is afraid that she isn't doing anything worthwhile with the life she has been given. To the Café and Back every day of the god damn week, she is weary of how each hour she lives merely bleeds into the next, indiscernibly, like words on wet newspaper.

'I'm that tribe in the Amazon, with no concept of time,' she says. 'There are these people who've never needed to measure dates, never invented how, and they just do the same thing over and over. Building the same house, weaving the same basket, eating the same moose or whatever, until it's finished. Or they die.'

'It sounds idyllic,' I say, and I mean it.

'I saw it on a show.'

2. Lorrie had been taking sedatives.

'Ah,' I said, keeping my eyes to the floor. I tell her that I also took prescriptions but she is not really interested in anything that doesn't catalyse serenity.

She feels that the sedatives contrived bouts of confidence, that they did the check-ups on her psychic mechanisms, that they tweaked, and prodded, and re-balanced the mess.

She had been prescribed a-couple-a-day after the removal of her wisdom teeth, two months ago. Then she started taking them for migraines. For insomnia. Also, when doing the laundry. The sedatives apparently had depression side effects, so she picked up some anti-depressants from her friend who was a pharmacist. These apparently had the side effect of erectile dysfunction, but that was okay. The human body is a magical thing.

3. Lorrie was worried about her boyfriend, who never took anything in their relationship seriously. He was a callow man: didn't want to live in her

apartment, didn't want to see her more than three times a week, wanted to be free, always went out on weekends, never called. She wasn't spying on him, but she once saw him with his arm around this woman (this absolute slut) from work, when they were meant to be getting quote-unquote quiet drinks, to quote-unquote build team spirit, so she went up to him, and you know what she did? She pushed him from behind and threw a drink on the crotch of his trousers all symbolic like in the movies and that evening he came to her house and she screamed at him and she cried and promised repercussions but then they settled down and he kissed her on the cheek and then the mouth and then they took their clothes off. Why couldn't he be more like you, Phil? You're different. You're so nice. You're special.

My heart is in my ears when she says this, though I can see that Lorrie has been biting the inside of her lip at every pause. I am, nevertheless, still nervous/elated.

'Don't worry about him,' I say.

To comfort her, I touch her on the shoulder. She, surprised, recoils, and so I, surprised, recoil. We repel each other upon contact, like magnets.

'I'm sorry I did that.'

'I brought it up', she says, sobbing. 'It's my fault.'

The moon is already out at four. The setting sun shimmers across the Pacific, leaving coins of light on the tide. Facing the sea, I shut my eyes and its dwindling heat scrabbles across my face with spider feet. I listen to the sea, during times like these, and it always has something insightful to say. When Lorrie makes her excuses to leave, the last thing she notices is a small, sad boy, with his eyes closed tightly. He is holding a metal detector and he seems to be muttering, though no one is around to listen.

Sheenal Singh | # ROLLER DERBY

To be a grrrl

Sleek, sexy and mysterious in tight black leather and stilettos, weapons in places your hands will never go—she's an Assassin. But if I were one, I'd add a splash of harlot scarlet to the wardrobe and swap my stilettos for a pair of wicked wheels. As for weaponry ... see this body? You're looking at it.

They're aggressive, competitive and tough, wrapped up in booty shorts, piercings, tattoos and fishnets. They're comfortable in this irony. It is, after all, the point of being a derby girl for the Sydney City Assassins.

Welcome to Sydney's roller derby.

Game day, and it's a war

Princess Leia, with her crowning glory curled neatly around her ears, offers her greetings at the door. Fish and chips and cigarette smoke mingle pleasantly in the crisp afternoon air outside the Hordern Pavilion.

A motley crew of spectators gather around the black drums and chairs scattered around the courtyard. Mothers jostle toddlers and talk animatedly in small circles. Recalcitrant twenty-somethings in black trench coats swirling about tight black jeans talk music and mild expletives in a cloud of thick smoke.

Then you step inside the cavernous track. Strobe lights, pounding music and a handful of Darth Vaders and Imperial Stormtroopers trawling the wooden floor. Tonight's theme: 'roller' wars. They're feminising the legendary saga. George Lucas, eat your heart out.

A gathering of curious voyeurs sit cross-legged around the track. Only a white line separates them from the skaters. It's affectionately called 'suicide seating'.

A little girl putters around amongst the seats, blonde ringlets alive around her face, a dummy poised carefully in her mouth. Another precocious child struts inside, vuvuzela dangling threateningly from her chubby fingers. A burly man in thick-framed glasses, jeans and a sports coat—polyester, of course—juggles a trio of beers in his hands as he cuts a swath through the crowd on remarkably light feet. Roller derby is a place of many contradictions. It hasn't quite figured itself out in Sydney yet.

More of a culture than a sport, it was a genuine pastime in the 1930s, when male and female skaters would play to over 55,000 fans. It then made a comeback in 1970s as a female fight club. Bouts were highly stylised with fake stunts and deliberate violence set on banked tracks; it's a sexier, fetishised version of World Wildlife Fund.

Somewhere in Texas, the local punk scene reappropriated the sport to defy its sullied association with commercialism in the 1970s. Today it's come back with a vengeance—flat-track grassroots and, so far, for women only. In 2007, the culture caught up with Sydney when the Hordern Pavilion opened its doors again to roller derby. This time, it was about women owning and playing the game. It would never own them again.

'The spectacle and entertainment is all good,' says Gold Coast derby girl Adele 'Deli Slicer' Pavlidis. '[But] it's about being a "grrrl" not a "girl".'

As derby film-maker Phoebe Hart puts it, this is a place for 'the smoky vixen, nerd babe, pretty girly girl, tough bitch'. Part fantasy, part feminism.

The Assassins sashay out. Aprilla the Hun, Winnie Bruise, Captain Ratz and a host of other quasi-Jedis outfitted in tees and teeny red satin shorts, brandishing red lightsabers postured and preened. Lithe bodies dip and sway around the track. It's dizzying, but you can't quite look away.

The Canberra Vice City Rollers follow suit with slightly bigger and (darnn it) multicoloured lightsabers.

Calls fade in and out from the crowd: 'Take it off! We want some biff!'

Referees sweep on too, one pairing his wheels with a coquettishly flighty kilt (whether in true Scot spirit or not remains a lingering mystery).

Some of the girls have strapped remote sensors to their helmets which feed maps of their bodies onto plasma screens. This is BloodBath, a live installation artwork spearheaded by Australian artist Linda Dement. She's been trying to find the ultimate way to expose derby as a culture where women break away from the particulars of revered femininity, where their physicality and independence come out to play.

'I love the wild-girl rough, daring, edgy play of it all,' Linda muses. 'When I was younger I used to do wrestling, in jelly or spaghetti or mud … It was incredibly fun to be violent in a playful but risky way. I feel this same energy in roller derby, but on a much larger scale.'

Each game or 'bout' lasts thirty minutes with one and a half minute 'jams' in which the team 'jammer' attempts to pass through the opposition to score points. Both teams are highly tactical units—pivots, blockers, jammers—all working in tandem to make every jam worthwhile. The pivot, bearing a striped helmet, is the tactician. She controls the pace, direction and defence line. The jammers, who balance themselves en pointe, are the key point scorers.

The crowd cheers at every bump and fall. Every once in a while a girl crawls off the track clutching various body parts in pain. In that moment there is a generous mingling of anxiety and exhilaration. This strange emotion forges a fragile, temporary intimacy between players and audience.

There's a minute and a half left on the clock. The scores are tied. Assassins' jammer, Carrie 'Winnie Bruise' Grace, takes a hit and is knocked onto one foot an inch from the line. If she falls now the Assassins lose the game.

'I somehow recovered, used every single muscle within my body to pull it back,' Winnie recalls.

'Game over.'

How to be an assassin: training

They meet outside the gates of a suburban high school. The girls are adorned with an assortment of tattoos, coloured hair and roller bling (including a derby knuckleduster-esque ring). A few cigarettes and a bit of small talk—'fluffy bathmats are way better than sandpapery ones'—and we're ready to go in. Winnie gives me a politely curious look.

'Just coming to perve on us?'

'Pretty much.'

We walk inside the lonely gymnasium. A makeshift flat-track marked out with beige-coloured tape curves awkwardly around the wooden floor.

Shorts, tights, tees, knee-pads, wrist-pads, elbow-pads and skates are strewn aside as they casually coiffe themselves in roller gear. There is scattered conversation amidst the comforting sounds of ripping velcro. It's a familiar routine—clunky black Assassin armour that fits like a second skin.

A willowy blue-eyed woman with dreadlocks gathered together in a loose braid takes centre stage. She's Mental Elf—an Assassins trainer.

Wheels squeal peevishly against the wooden grain at dizzying speed. The sound is incredible; it's as loud and commanding as a well-oiled train sweeping through a station, gathering speed and whipping deep, hollow timbres of vibration through brick and mortar.

Mental Elf declares this training session to be one of the lighter options on the four-day menu. It took three hours. I look at the thirsty and sweaty girls; could have fooled me.

They break out into smoky peals of laughter and throw around choice words as they duck, weave and whip past each other. There is an easy camaraderie to be found here.

I want in.

The grrrls

It's the closest I've ever come to being a part of the iconic joint-smoking circle on *That 70s show*. There's a certain pleasure in using words like 'dude' and 'awesome' in adult conversation.

And they do like to talk. A lot.

Winnie Bruise rushes in from work. She chose her derby name by running a competition between her friends. April 'Aprilla the Hun' Agnew, looking every inch like the professional woman that she is, settles onto the couch. Her husband-to-be came up with her alter ego in the shower. Tiffany 'Captain Ratz' Knight laughs. Her husband, a police officer, christened her with the name before she became a derby girl.

'Cop code for someone who is totally nuts or bat-shit crazy is "Captain Ratz",' she explains. 'Everybody thinks it's a mousy superhero.'

The name stuck.

I ask them what roller derby means to them.

Carrie answers with remarkable aplomb. 'It's a fun, fast-paced, athletic all-female contact sport within a supportive derby community.'

'What did you say? I fell asleep!' Tiffany replies.

April chimes in, 'Or is it the smacking of the bitches?'

'It's the smacking of the bitches within a supportive derby community,' Carrie resigns herself to agree.

Carrie is one of those really cool chicks. Rakishly short hair, black boots, jeans and a t-shirt, she also had a street-cred job at a music store go with it all. Always the athlete, she was completely hooked after her first roller derby experience and now trains four times per week.

Tiffany has got California girl charm in spades. According to her, she had no life before she joined the roller derby in 2009.

'Coming from another country, I didn't have any friends … I got up at one o'clock and Dr Phil came on, followed by Ellen, and they were my friends … roller derby really gave me a life.'

By day, she works at a private members' club watching politicians and hoity-toity types sip champagne. 'I sit there in a polyester suit with a name tag and have to cater to these people. I'm kind of this doormat at work, and when I go to derby, it's like bad-ass hit-'em-up chill-cool. Half the members would be disgusted if they knew what my life was like.'

'God, I don't talk about derby at work,' April declares, 'because they're lawyers.'

She joined the league with six girls in 2007, when it all took place in a basketball court at the back of some high school.

Three years later, the girls are key players in Sydney's all-star Assassins outfit. The Pavilion sells out when they take to the track. They train and play damn hard to put on a good show.

Falling flat on your backside is part of the thrill of the game for audiences, but at times it's easy to overlook the hours of training required to fall properly and take others down according to the rules of the game.

'They enjoy the big spills but they're not going to get off if a girl goes down,' says Tiffany. 'I don't think they realise how much training it takes to play well without hurting yourself and other people.'

'Some girls get the shits if they trip and fall. But you know what? You're playing fuckin' roller derby.'

Carrie has come as close as one can to breaking one's ribs; it hurt to breathe for a month. April ruptured a ligament in her knee. She was out for seven.

Tiffany helpfully remembers one of the more interesting injuries in April's career. 'Hey, didn't you get a skate in a ... dark area?'

April, somewhat peeved, spills. 'Yeah, I did get a skate to the "vagine" once. It really hurts. Don't do it.'

I wonder if that's why men don't play the game.

'Oh god, could you imagine!' laughs April.

'They'd wear a cup. Don't they wear it in all contact sports?' That's Carrie. Tiffany, displeasure written all over her face: 'They wear it for bloody paintball!'

Short of wiggling on booty shorts and fishnets for a team, men still play an important role in the derby as referees, coaches and volunteers.

'They just want to be involved because it's a lot of fun, and a lot of them don't get to see their girlfriends or wives if they don't turn up,' explains Carrie.

It seems everybody has given a piece of themselves to the game.

Since its heyday in the 1970s, the sensuality of the game has played a heavy hand in developing the identity of the sport. Some see it as an essential part of the sport while others mentally reduce the culture to sex alone.

'I think we're all big characters, with or without the name,' says Tiffany.

'We're comfortable in what we wear and we aren't going to sex it up to sell tickets. We know how much work we put in. They can whack off when they take a shower when they think of Aprilla's name, but that's them.'

In April's opinion, at least the sport isn't as discerning as lingerie football in the USA where only model-proportioned girls can play.

'The thing about roller derby is that, yeah, we might be playing up feminine sexuality in all its forms, but at no time do we try to define or stereotype it.'

The Sydney league has grown to support more than eighty players and a community of volunteers.

'[People] don't really get it, so they turn up to watch what the fuck it is and then they're just hooked, because it's so neat and different and fun and fringy and shreddy and fishnetty,' Tiffany reels off. It's hard to pinpoint the appeal of this chaotic, athletic, risqué sporting culture.

The girls are kooky and creative. Sure, they can pull on their tongue-in-cheek personalities and put the moves on, but what really matters is that they're always who they are and who they want to be.

Dark and dangerous Assassins this year, but they'll be rainbows and glittery unicorns the next.

Nicholas Fahy | # CHOICES

I hold in my hand several gold coins
I no longer need.
Would you like them?

Nicholas Fahy | # JUNE EYES

Eyes like a candle
Flicker upon me still,
A violent blue, a shudder,
A fateful thrill,
But a moment it lasts
Entreats me still
To the freedom I find—
Her eyes: a lovely window sill.

Nicholas Fahy | # THE AESTHETICS OF BEAUTY

The butterfly's beauty
Lies in infinite fragility,
Its wings concede to the breath of Wind;
At the Wind's word he ceases to be free.

The garden's beauty
Lies in eternal tranquillity,
Though Age may creep and steal its flowers
It is a garden everlastingly.

A girl's beauty
Lies in her delicate sorrows;
For while Innocence may take his share
Her eyes will always shine with the horizons of tomorrow.

Justin Pen | DEAD MEAT

As the lights dimmed, faces fell like flies struck by a swat.

The camera weaved slowly between the four silhouetted figures. Sweat beads trickled from foreheads onto greasy faces, like rain drops on a blood-soaked corpse in a dirty back alley. Someone's life was on the line, there was no ambiguity about it. Whip-pan to a rotund man in a proud black blazer, a spotless white shirt and a gaudy, crimson cravat.

'I'm sorry Sarah,' he paused, as if allowing her to pray. 'You are … dead meat.'

Tears spurted from her eyes like blood from a mangled tourniquet. The remaining contestants embraced, celebrating their survival.

Pete squatted and motioned his camera towards Sarah, the lone weeping angel. The overhead spotlight shone down—an unrelenting artificial sun, a cheap trick from 1950s noir. The harsh, unrestrained lighting exposed her grief. Pete's job was just to get it on film. The upshot was going to make a great promo. 'Who knows?' he mused. Maybe he'd save the reel for his portfolio.

'And then there were five,' declared the portly man. 'See you all Sunday on, Australia's Top Cook!'

It was a sober Saturday afternoon when he walked into the Top Cook compound. He lazily scanned his ID badge, 'Peter Wolfe—Cameraman, Clearance Level 2,' before ambling down the western entrance. He yawned. It was a rehearsal for Sunday's live segment, 'Under Pressure'—no one got in or out until the two hours elapsed.

This meant another afternoon dealing with the show's remaining prima donnas. He'd make the rounds as each practised scrunching up their face while sautéing, basting or baking. Pete had witnessed the whole staged canvas of the human condition week after week after week—it all came down to variations of quivering lips, batting eyelids and flaring nostrils. The right combination could spell grief, panic or triumph. Sometimes simultaneously.

All the stationary cameras had been deactivated—cost-cutting measures. The network executives had figured it would be cheaper to get a dogsbody with a handheld camera to film the dry runs. Week after week, the contestants would play the tapes back, poring over every frame to see when to time their tears and when to blink them back.

Pete began his tour of duty with a routine inspection of ground zero. He strolled through the Cooking Arena, looking for an angle, an edge he hadn't yet explored. Worm's eye, bird's-eye, high angle, low angle, Dutch tilt, close-up, Italian close-up. Twenty-seven years old, still wet behind the ears from film school and already he was trapped in a swamp of boredom.

His eyes wandered towards the sauna and his feet were quick to follow. Pete wasn't too fond of any of the contestants, but Nigel was always a laugh. He wore a claret-coloured beret, genuinely appreciated silent film, and was an avid member of a barbershop quartet. Every other week, he would hear Nigel gently humming 'My Wild Irish Rose' to the four silent, steaming, wooden walls.

But not this Saturday.

Nigel's beret sat on the clothes hanger, staring at Pete like an eager puppy. He gave a wry smile and pulled it over his fringe, gently propping his camera up.

'Nigel, I hope you don't mind. I'm borrowing your cap!' he shouted, cheekily.

As he pried apart the Finnish double doors, his smirk dissipated just as quickly as the first jets of vapour escaped into the corridor. Pete hastened towards his camera and strapped it around his left hand. His eyeballs verged on popping out of their sockets. Nigel lay motionless; sprawled on the floor like a steamed salmon—blotchy, puffy, pink and tender.

Pete couldn't stomach getting any closer to the still fresh corpse, so he zoomed in instead. Gentle pan across the body. From the corner of the frame, he noticed something out of place. A few feet from Nigel lay a short, sharp cooking knife covered by a thin sheet of condensation and blood.

Shaky cam, as Pete rushed back to the Cooking Arena. His eyes darted between the bedrooms and the exit. The doors were automated. They would only open when—Pete glanced at the large clock overhead.

3:26 pm.

There was no manual override. He was locked in for another hour and a half.

He was a pig on a spit. Pete was sweating, burning on all sides as the room spun around like a ghastly rotisserie. His camera drew him to the bedroom despite the objections from his legs and chest. The camcorder had become an extension of his left hand, far more curious, more courageous than he was.

Pete did a mental head check as he dragged himself down the northern corridor. Nigel was in the sauna. That left Duncan 'The Kitchen Warrior' and 'Family' Jim. He planted his feet by the right side of the door and leant in with his camera. Tilt cam. Through the digital screen, the scene suggested little. The room was a mess but the cooks were world-class slobs. He cautioned closer, canvassing the room.

He stood by the bed marked 'Sarah', hovering over the mass like a coroner in a morgue. Gently peeling back the navy blanket, Pete found a pair of mottled white pillows soaking, marinating in bright red blood.

There were no bodies in any of the beds and only Sarah's was drenched in blood.

Soft little footsteps echoed from the hallway, like a lamb trotting about.

Pete stumbled into the break room still dazed and weary from the sight of red, the smell of rust and salt, the tomato soup texture of blood. He was refused a reprieve. Sprawled over the pool table was 'Family' Jim. He was a stay-at-home father, a dorky dad, a single parent. Jim cracked bad jokes but made up for them with an impeccable ratatouille.

'Family' Jim lay belly up across the pool table, a knife in his chest.

Duncan had a cult following in the Australian-Scottish community. He was the Cooking Warrior, the Kitchen Braveheart, the Fiery Red. Critics drew comparisons to Gordon Ramsey, but Duncan rejected any similarities with an acid tongue.

'Don't use that name in my kitchen,' he'd bellow. Duncan was very superstitious. 'Don't say his name,' he'd warn. 'Just call him, the Scottish Chef.'

It wasn't the Scot that was traipsing about. Duncan lay slumped across the floor in a shallow puddle of red. A vicious gash ran across his neck. There had to have been a lot of blood. The Kitchen Warrior looked much paler, much thinner already.

Pete thought of the bloodied pillows and the bodiless bed. Someone had tried to clean up. The carpet was still damp, but nowhere near as wet as it was supposed to be. He spotted a roll of paper towels left behind from tiny little lamb-like footsteps which lead straight back to the Cooking Arena.

She was a vision in immaculate white.

Her buttons shone, menacingly opaque under the bright hot lights. He laid the camera gently on the table top as a peace offering.

'That's a fine first start,' Sarah hissed. She squeezed the butcher's knife, tight in her right hand. She had a rattlesnake's grip on the wide, blunt blade.

Fear built up in Pete's throat like toxic phlegm till he coughed, 'W-Why?'

He tried to stall. He looked above to see the glowing clock face.

3:49 pm.

She crept closer to him. Her gaze was unflinching.

'You're going to be another mess,' she spat the word with venom, 'that I'll need to tidy up. There's still a spill or two in the break room I believe.'

He remembered her time on the show. She was obsessive compulsive when it came to keeping clean. Her infant son had passed from a staph infection. Sarah blamed herself even though it wasn't her fault. There had always been a vulnerability, an intensity, an authenticity to her pain. Something he had always caught on camera. Something Pete had never really seen before.

'There's a spot!' he cried, pointing at her wrist. 'You've got red on your sleeve!'

She shrieked and ran for the sink. 'Damn spot. Out! Get out!' She threw the knife into the basin. It slid smoothly against the stainless steel.

Sarah clapped her palms together under the running faucet. Pete lunged for the knife, snatched it from the sink and held it firmly towards her.

'Why?' he protested. 'Why?'

Her voice chilled to a monotone. 'For my son,' she muttered softly, barely audible over the gushing tap.

'I killed them for my son. They had no heartache. I had to win, I had to. For my son. A geriatric who had never felt suffering. A doting father who had never felt loss. A dumb caricature who wasn't even real. For my son. My son ...'

She leapt at Pete with wet hands and wet face. The knife in his hand met the pain in her chest. Warm blood and cool steel. Sarah collapsed in his arms.

'I see him,' she groaned through the pain. 'I see my son.'

5:00 pm.

The doors unsealed themselves.

Pete sat shaking by the kitchen cabinets. Camera strapped to his hand. He pressed 'play' for the umpteenth time. There was no visual. But he could hear it.

'That's a fine start', hissed the video camera.

Joel Mak | SKETCH OF A(N) (ALBANY)BUS STATION

Dedicated to Lucy, who knows what it's like to be stranded in bus stations

Four hour layover in a
decrepit
    bus station
    in
    Albany, NY
        yes that New York
           that deceptively huge state
        with an income gap actually
           mirroring that of LA one might wager
    North
    of
    Poughkeepsie, NY

There's a pattern of beauty in the toponymy of New York City
    Soulless names of referral
        Downtown Midtown Uptown
        Chinatown
        or
        Little Italy
    Soulless street names
        8th Ave. & 42nd St.
    but look elsewhere!

Binghampton
& Syracuse
& Rochester
& even Saratoga Springs!
& my worn down Greyhound Station is on
Hamilton St.
surrounded (ironically) by
Liberty St.

But this is Albany, the bus station reflecting perhaps
(for I have never ventured out of it)
the city of Albany
& if it does, this is what I see

low ceiling previously I s'pose a glistening white
but now dirtied murky grey
tiled flooring a musky mixture of yellow & grey
a colour not unknown to those who've
had a drink too many.

the benches are a lazy blue
chosen by a lazy interior designer
who went for the common blue
the known blue
the familiar blue
of commercial paint

& there are perhaps eight of them
divided in two rows
two facing the same side
the same wall
which divides us, the commuters from

the outside
the buses
the pollutants
another two facing the other way
at me
or past me
at a 'food court'
(which I'll come to later

because this conversation I hear on my left has captured my interest
not least because she is salient
in size
& voice
& sobs)

fr. she is stuck in Albany I deduce
a missed bus (& consequently a 12-hour wait)(this at ten in the night)
(so y'll understand her distress)
(coupled with the nothingness that the station provides—
fr. look around!
& y'll see the blank empty spaces of the floor
which the benches do not take up
cz. Albany council members have already decided that
no one will be boarding buses in Albany
even those on the way to Montréal
well, they're hardly going to *faire rouler l'économie*
& that food court (manned by a heavy African American lady jovial
but asks you what y'want in the same tone in which someone asks you
who y'd vote for)
with a replicable menu
as stale as its offerings
of burgers chips and fried fish fillets

cold sandwiches
    cold salads
minuscule fruit cups
    artificial colouring
larger refillable soda cups
& the same food court sells
instant noodles!
    & instant!
fixes to momentary needs
      because the same councillors know that we will not survive a
four hr ordeal
    in Albany
        or a ten-hour monotonous drive upstate
    with broken earphones
    or broken iPods
    or depleted batteries
    & so they provide us with them
—this food court with three tables seating four each (and another
two seating two)
    with its swivel chairs that swivel only one side
& entertainment in the form of arcade games
    giving us the chance to win stuffed pink rabbits (with disconcerting
smiles)
    or beat a programmed race car driver
all providing a digitalised rainbow to the backdrop of Albany
    NY
(in these places of nourishment I find that the aim is to fill yrself
    and leave
    as qwkly as psbl—
just like the mother who sits across her young son
    reaches over to wipe tomato sauce from the left of her son's lips
    and adds too:

quickly finish yr food!)
& so our lady sobs on the phone to someone who (hopefully) cares
   till
       the battery runs out—.

the PA plays top 40 music
   in the food court
     but loud enough to extend outside
       for the benched travellers
       (most of them chins on chests anyway
       with their earphones
          personal worlds
           & if the lady sitting next to me is really into her magazine
             on Angelina Jolie
             and similar stars
             then she's not hearing Beyoncé belting it out either)

I've got two more hours here
   the tailbone aches
     against an uncompromising bench
   but man's worst enemy is boredom
     or waiting for time to pass
     in disinterested bus stations manned by impartial bilingual staff
       (fr. *todo el mundo habla español aquí*)
       (even as most of us head to Montréal)

in quietness sounds are AMPLIFIED
   such as the fake HAHAs of staff
   in reply to mild jokes
     so is the WAILING of a baby
     or the slam of the door as drivers move in and out of the terminal
       (& when they open the GROANS

of the buses
—perhaps unwilling to undertake another
ten hour journey
or just shaking at the prospect of US immigration)
I've half a mind to initiate conversation
with someone, anyone
for sanity

but I'm in Albany, NY
(or rather, because I am unashamedly well-travelled enough to notice
this:
I'm in a Greyhound station
with its architecture meant for the decades of past
now unconducive to socialisation
—has not kept up with the times
or perhaps not attempted to at all
and similar pictures one'll find in
Memphis, TN
or Philadelphia, PA)
& the aim is to get on the bus and to will the driver to get you to yr
destination as fast as possible

—just as I climb the steps of my bus
after handing the conductor my ticket
& personally stowing my luggage under the bus
I ask *y'doin alright chief?*
to which he responds *sure am!*
& I add *well safe drive and stay awake eh?*
& left Albany
NY.

Joel Mak | SKETCH OF AN ORDINARY (BEAUTIFUL) DAY

sky; it is
    water colour blue (all corners of the white canvas blue, too)
    with drips of white
        not enough to rain on this parade

housewife
  flapping a towel
    on the balcony
before draping it over the railings

old lady
    leaning
    pushing forward
        on a trolley
not that i want it
    but I wonder where she keeps her wallet

birds
    flying in seemingly random directions
    if you draw an imaginary line
        tracing their movement as they fly from point A to B via C
        against the blue
        i bet all y'd
    get

wouldn't look much diffrn't
    to hair on the floor
        of a barber shop

cars
    with windows down

kids
    school hats
    in sandboxes
    designing castles
        (or ancient infrastructure)

the postie
    in his bright neon green
    competing with traffic lights for attention
plops a letter in number 12
a parcel in number 14
    apologises to number 16
        leaves a collection notice
skips number 18
    number 20 hasn't had mail for the past week
number 22
    a new ms. Jones
        's got mail for the past month now
            now rather frequent
    (mr. Lee has a new partner)
number 24 a letter
a stack of junk mail in number 26
    the box is so full that
        the envelopes protrude
            brown and white

our postie tries to stuff in this letter
    it crumples
    but it's not his fault
postie gets on the bike again
    swings over to number 11 on the other side of the street
      he restarts
and before he says hi to the terrier on the lawns of number 15
    he spots the housewife of number 13
       who's just had a baby
       the recycle bins
          not properly closed
          reveal IKEA boxes
             containing what once perhaps was
             a crib

leaving the postie
it's two in the afternoon
    in thirty minutes the kids leave the public schools
      end within an end.

Shaun Colnan | ABODE & ABROAD

I have seen azure streams leading to crystalline shores,
Jungles brimming with reptiles and insects.
I've seen nature humming in cycles about me
But no greater solace comes than from what I've found in my abode.
As I walk, the air is wintry but the leaves are covered,
Imbued with an ambrosial dew
And still the autumn auburn hue.

—It's true: I've heard sonorous symphonies
Far away, abroad
But peace is creeping along
The vines along the rock wall.
Simple solitude slips
down my drive,
Carrying the leaves into the drains
But not before leaving their mark
(though not indelible)
Tattooed on the concrete.

I can smell smoke slithering about my senses
But it's okay.
The fires haven't returned.
It's just the fireplaces ignited by weary lovers
Who still entwine themselves to keep warm,
To keep out of the storm.

The valley is filled with sunlight now
—But not for long.
Soon the quarter-crescent-moon will have to do,
Illuminating in slivers the ashen-tiled-roofs
And casting an eye on the shivering white-brick-cottages
To make sure they make it through the night.

I will be quiet in my bed,
Wishing I could remain young forever
(or otherwise)
Dreaming I could grow old in my abode and grasp these memories always
with vitality
And when I'm done I'll store them in jam jars on a shelf in the garage
And I'll say to myself,
Just before I've sealed the glinting things

—Just a pinch of salt
And they'll last for an eternity
They'll outlive my organs & my flesh
They'll make fools of my bones
And until that house collapses

Or until they free my soul,
They'll live on in those jam jars like diamonds,
Recalling—as wind gusts rust the street lamps
And the whorls strip the trees of leaves
And carry the remnants into the languid valley—recalling what I did
abroad
& what I did in my abode.

Pristine Ong | AFRICAN THEATRE

Between dreams and reality:
The African Company performs *Richard III*, 1821

*Our strong arms be our conscience, swords our law, March on, join
bravely, let us to it pell-mell; If not to heaven, then hand in hand to
hell.—Richard III*, William Shakespeare

As the early decades of the nineteenth century ushered slavery out of
New York, the experiments through which the city's African-Americans
tested the limits of their freedom would intensify dramatically. One of
these experiments was William Brown's audacious creation of the first
black theatre company. Riding on the waves of cultural invigoration and
driven by slavery's impending demise, the African Company would open
up the stage to black actors with its production of *Richard III* in 1821. The
staging of the first African-American production of a Shakespearean play
by non-white Americans created a very public challenge to the assumption
that public space and cultural production in New York was exclusively
white. The apocalyptic reproduction of *Richard III* would be echoed in
the tumultuous state of contemporary New York. Just as Shakespeare
depicted a past in which violence governed people's lives, the African
Company's expropriation of the play re-enacted the violent exclusion
and discrimination experienced by Africans in New York. Shakespeare's
portrayal of the human body, endangered by the struggle for sovereign
power, mirrored the state of New York's political landscape as 'whiteness'
was established as a condition for suffrage. In effect, the African Company
mounted the play as a cultural protest which was driven by Charles Taft's
representation of the scheming king, S. Welsh's enlivened Lady Ann and,
most importantly, by Brown's attempt to institutionalise a black public

space in the outskirts of New York and in direct competition with the dominant Park Theatre.

African-American suffrage

From the first time the African Company raised its curtains on Richard III, the liminal space of the stage—despite the constant mobility of the theatre—provided a forum in New York City for black actors and audiences to openly congregate and socialise. As indicated by a playbill for one of the performances, 'Mr. Brown has spared neither time nor expense in rendering this Entertainment agreeable to Ladies and Gentlemen of Color'. The National Advocate observed 'The black dandys and dandizettes, after attending meeting, occupied the sidewalks of Broadway and slowly lounged toward their different homes. As their numbers increased, and their consequence strengthened; partly from high wages, high living and the elective franchise; it was considered necessary to have a place of amusement for them exclusively.'

The formation of a commercialised communal space around the staging of a play highlighted a growing, but heretofore, unanswered need in New York. On one hand, the city's black population was growing rapidly, with a 40 percent increase between 1810 and 1830. On the other hand, they were unwelcome at major entertainment centres despite being able to afford entertainment. Just as the *National Advocate*'s report pointed to the phenomenon of a minority of blacks maintaining a public profile, Brown's staging of *Richard III* would assertively stamp their visibility across New York life and culture.

In many ways, Brown's decision to debut with the final play from Shakespeare's War of the Roses history cycle also reflected the transformation of race relations in New York. Citing Stuart Hall's contention that cultural identity is a 'matter of "becoming" as well as being', Marvin McAllister locates Brown's theatrical venture within contemporary struggles with plurality. Specifically, the staging of *Richard III* was aware of the developments regarding New York State's constitutional convention, which had proposed disenfranchising black voters. In New York City, the political debate took a rhetorical form that dramatised the connection between the black vote and Afro-New Yorkers' interest in theatre. Reporting that Brown opened *Richard III* shortly after police closed his ice cream garden at the African Grove, the *National Advocate* wrote that 'by virtue of the great charter that declares "all men are equal" and after several nightly caucuses, [the African Company] resolved to get up a play'. By referring to the Declaration of Independence and parliamentary images like 'caucuses', the newspaper argued that for black New Yorkers, theatre-making was a political act which enabled them to participate in nation-building. McAllister's emphasis on cultural 'becoming' highlights the important aspirational quality that characterised cultural productions like *Richard III*. Staged in tandem with political developments on prejudiced conditions of suffrage, the daring action of colour-blind casting would challenge the racial generalisation that visibly divided New York City.

Adaptation of *Richard III*

As debates over limiting the black vote continued, the African Company's adaptation of *Richard III* asserted the rights of black citizens by laying claim to cultural equality. On the play's opening night, Charles Taft soliloquised, 'Now is de vinter of our discontent made glorious by de son of New-York.' As exemplified by Taft's performance, the African Company manipulated Shakespeare's language, transforming speech into a creolised form. By integrating 'Brother William' into their theatre practice, African-American actors staked a claim to a shared cultural ownership between white and black Americans. Effectively, the African Company unravelled the previously accepted cultural boundaries between white artistic practitioners and black spectators in New York.

The African Company framed their creative response to their hard-won freedom in terms of the cyclical violence that characterised the civil war in *Richard III*. With the 1827 deadline for manumission looming, the company expropriated the story of Richard III's usurpation of peace and power to depict the freedom borne of violence in New York. In particular, Welsh's spirited representation of the bereaved Lady Ann reflected the condition of female slaves in New York. The production focused on the underlying exchange of property in Lady Ann's marriage to Richard III by adapting it to reflect the enslavement of black females in New York.

Although perceived as 'incorrect' by the *National Advocate* review, Welsh's violent characterisation of Lady Ann's encounter with Richard III paralleled the reality of violent resistance—in the form of arson, assault and poisonings—led by female slaves in New York against their masters. Rejecting the traditional portrayal of Lady Ann as subdued by her grief, Welsh instead sustained her performance with 'violent action, such as seizing the king by his wool, shaking him furiously, and finally dashing him on the earth'. In effect, Welsh's energetic conception reflected the defiance with which female slaves struggled for their freedom. That Richard still dominated Lady Ann at the end of the scene is testament to the precarious freedom experienced by slaves in New York.

But did it make noise?

Just as artistic intervention may expose the limits of American democratic ideals, the African Company's production of *Richard III* unveiled white Americans' intolerance for the visibility of black occupation of New York public space. In noting that the theatre 'made some noise in this city', one New York newspaper characterised the African Company's activities with a sense of forcefulness. That this highly visible black public presence was at odds with white New Yorkers' expectation that freed blacks would 'fade quietly into the background' is demonstrated by the mobility of the African Theatre. As a result of the limited space available to the company, throughout the 1821–1822 season of *Richard III* the play was performed in three separate locations: the upper apartments of the African Grove on Thomas Street, in the undeveloped lots of Mercer and Bleecker Streets and finally in Hampton's Hotel, next door to Stephen Price's dominant Park Theatre. Concomitant to the feeling among white Americans that they were losing control over New York was Stephen Price's fear of the African Company's displacement of the Park Theatre's authority as New York's major commercial theatre. In response to Brown's audacious staging of *Richard III* in Hampton Hotel in 1822, Price manipulated the police to interfere with the production and arrest the players. The *National Advocate* satirised the event, reporting that the actors 'pleaded so hard in blank verse, and promised never to act Shakespeare again'. In light of the fact that no arrests appeared in court records, the *National Advocate*'s article may be read as an account of cultural confrontation driven by a misuse of legal power in New York. The arrests revealed the fallacy of the city's founding myth of being the egalitarian commercial and cultural capital of America.

References

Dewberry J (1982). The African Grove Theatre and Company. *Black American Literature Forum*, 16(4): 128–31.

Foucault M (2003). *Society must be defended.* Macey D (trans). London: Allen Lane.

McAllister M (2003). *White people do not know how to behave at entertainments designed for ladies & gentlemen of color: William Brown's African & American Theater.* Chapel Hill: University of Noth Carolina Press.

Odell George CD (1927–1949) *Annals of the New York stage.* New York: Columbia University Press.

Thompson G (1998). *A documentary history of the African Theatre.* Evanston, Illinois: Northwestern University Press.

Warner M (2001). A soliloquy 'lately spoken at the African Theatre': race and the public sphere in New York City, 1821. *American Literature,* 73(1): 1–46.

White S (1991). *Somewhat more independent: the end of slavery in New York City, 1770–1810.* Athens, Georgia: University of Georgia Press.

White S (2002). *Stories of freedom in black New York.* Cambridge, Massachusetts: Harvard University Press.

Paul Ellis | THE HOUR'S UP!

No one blames the Babylonians
For their legacy that is time.
We go along, get broken in
And minutes become just fine.

But take a minute just to think,
We have X fingers for a reason.
A compendium of tens, perfectly in sync;
Our tradition amounts to treason.

We decimalised the Sterling
And welcomed the pleasing Pence.
Why can't we say: Hour—'nough hurting,
We're having time in hundreds instead.

The time has come, the hour's up,
The sixties should be gone.
Let's set-up a modern measure,
That produces much less scorn.

Alexander Dorohokuplia |

These photographs document my suburb, Lewisham. This series of photographs remind us of social walls that are constructed. There is a continuing theme of separation in the work. There is disconnection between the viewer and the subject, and between the photographer and the subject. This is so even though the viewer has a clear sense of place and location in the photographs. They also have a documentary-esque feel that gives them honesty; the black-and-white format adds to this. This series screams that we are always outsiders looking in.

Nicholas Fahy | # SUNSET

Feng Guo | IN THE JUNGLE

Feng Guo is a fourth-year commerce and law student. Feng's art and photography has taken her all over the world, most recently her solo safari expedition through Kenya and Tanzania in Africa. This series attempts to capture the beauty and serenity of wild animals in their natural habitat. The blink of a zebra, a stampede of wildebeest, and the stare of a giraffe all serve to remind us of the ephemeral quality nature. We tend to forget that this stunning continent is home to a serious issue of animal poaching for ivory and skins, and that we must be active in the fight against this.

Peter Rolfe |

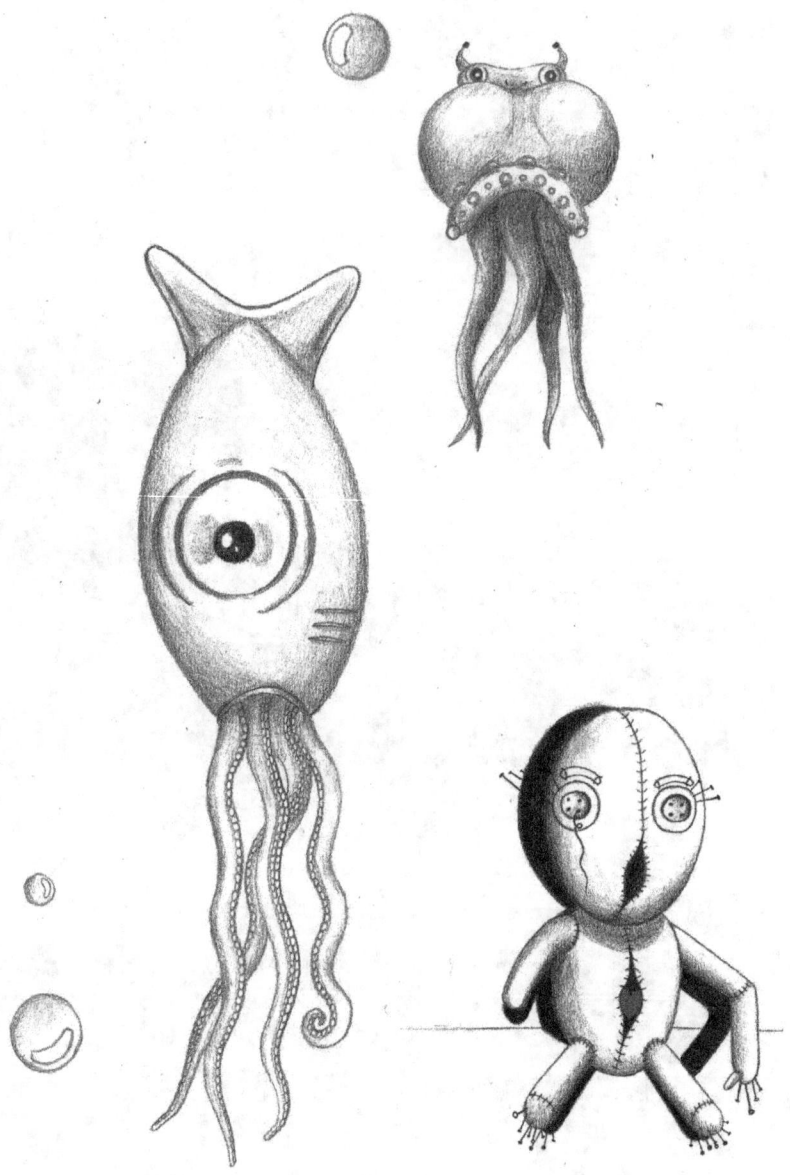

Danielle Chiaverini | # VIETNAM

These two photographs depict the variety and distinctness of two regions within Vietnam. They encapsulate a nation speeding forward, yet always remembering to meditate upon the past. The first image shows a family crammed on to a single moped in Hanoi, a highly common occurrence. The prevalence of scooters in Vietnam is certainly an unforgettable quirk. The second image is of the zooming, ever-present flow of traffic in the foreground contrasted against a cathedral in the background, in central Saigon. The high contrast and blurred aspects of these two pieces creates a sense of rapid pace and depicts the overwhelming nature of modern life and development in this country.

Duncan Idaho | # SOMETHING IN THE WAY

The sun is different from place to place. In Sydney the sun is dull and fuzzy and paints the city a pale yellow, rubbing away the natural edges of the world and reducing everything to a hazy shimmer. Hannah had left home at midday to walk through the park to a nearby shop for lunch. Her first step into the day had been met with a blush of heat, thick and drowsy that pressed against her skin and made her feel helpless. She hated the Sydney sun. If it were a man, she thought, it would resemble a loud fool who likes to lounge around and dress in black and smoke rolled cigarettes. Just like the loud fool who had tried to charm her at Bill's party Saturday night.

The whole evening she had pined for Bill Mayley. Bill was handsome and trim with a sharp jawline and a good smell. Not a false perfume smell but rather the sort of smell swimmers have after they've just come out of the pool. A lascivious chlorine smell Hannah loved to breathe in as she walked out of the change rooms. She'd taken to swimming every morning before university and she was never happier than when boxed in for an hour at the pool. What a thrill to feel her body smash into the water for the first time, and in that single apocalyptic second, feel as if the world had been annihilated, and she had split apart into space. For the next hour the world would be made low and distant, like the sound of a far-off animal howling in the night. Afterwards she'd climb out of the pool, her body light, breathless and tired and yet pulsating with strength. She would change out of her swimmers, her skin tight, cold and dancy, her pubic hair matted against her groin, and turn on the showers to feel a cold blast pummel her body and wash off the chlorine. Then she'd walk out into the world, like a horse at the starting gate, nervous with energy and stepping lightly on the earth.

There were many pleasures to be had boxed in at the pool. Special kinds of pleasure, pleasures that had come along suddenly when she was thirteen years old, and had stayed with her all the way to her present nineteenth year. It was a kind of pleasure that could make her feel light and breathless. Like after a hard swim. Bill Mayley made her feel this way. She had watched him once after training, his wet skin clean and pure, walking back to his towel, his red swimmers gripped tightly over his crotch. A tender pain tingled through her body, her thighs came together and later that night, as she lay in her bed with a pillow between her legs, she'd masturbated while thinking about him. They'd first met at the pool and the usual banter had (finally) led to a party invitation.

Come Saturday night, dressed in tight black jeans and a white singlet showing her black bra pushing up her breasts, Hannah left for the party nervous and taut, as if she were on the starting blocks with a loaded gun nearby. The way he looked at her she was sure he liked and wanted her. Like most young women in Sydney, Hannah was good-looking. With sharp green eyes, a suggestive face and a lithe and long nineteen-year-old body she would always catch men staring at her, and it pleased her up to a point. If they were handsome it was pleasurable, if they were ugly it was annoying. The ugly ones, she had quickly discovered, have tremendous difficulty in keeping themselves from staring. The manner of indifference they carry around with them is a hard mask to wear, and so often it falls apart and leaves them staring slack-jawed and fish-like at a girl like Hannah.

It's easy to tell when there's something off about a man. They'll stare at girls in a hurt, confused manner, like a spoilt child refused a candy bar, or a man who's just being caught downloading pornography at a public internet café. Men who find themselves in this situation have two options. They can either adopt a pose of pugnacious nonchalance as if to say: 'Yes, I'm a grown man and here I am in a public space downloading Bamboo Fantasies members only $29.95 a month and I'm not ashamed goddamn it all to hell, and if you've got a goddamn problem I'll sock you in the face!' Or they can go the more traditional route and fluster a bit and then pretend there's nothing odd or woeful about the whole position. It's a tough call to make and it will vary from man to man but in any case there's always a brief moment with both types when their eyes will spread open like scared fish and they'll look at you like a little boy whose lost his mother in a shopping centre. When this kind of look was directed at Hannah, as indeed it often was, she would squirm in discomfort and want them to go away and leave her alone.

But Bill didn't look at her like this. He'd look at her, she'd look at him, and then he'd break into a strong-wide smile, and Hannah's spine would curl with pleasure. Plenty of men in Sydney are ugly, so when a man like Bill looks at you like that, you've got to leap in at the first crack of the gun. Saturday night had come, and both Hannah and Bill expected that all this dreary circling round the edges would end. Hannah thought about his wet skin clean and pure and his red swimmers, and Bill thought about her pretty face and sharp green eyes. They were both of them tremendously excited. But almost as soon as Hannah had entered the fray on Saturday night she had become burdened with a louche man dressed in black and lisping sedition who trailed after her the whole evening. He was to begin with a mere irritation, like a single mosquito whining around your ear.

But his persistence, even after Hannah had clearly signaled to him that his presence was not welcome, altered him from a mere irritation into something altogether more sinister. All night whenever she tried to approach Bill he would either be engaged with someone, or this loud man would sidle up to her and start talking about his favourite bands and how America was an evil empire and Israel a terrorist state that ought to be boycotted. She soon became desperate. Initially she had been polite, and had looked him in the eye when he spoke to her, and pretended to be interested in what he had to say. But realising this was a form of encouragement, and men like this ought not to be encouraged, she had soon taken to looking at the ground or other people, when he started ranting. And even when she made her indifference and annoyance about as clear as she could without resorting to an outright proclamation of distaste, still he wouldn't leave her side. Every time she managed to escape, a few moments later, as sure as the sun, he would sidle up to her again, lean in with a smile and, like a wind-up toy, start ranting about America and Israel.

Her night, and her hopes about Bill's red swimmers had been ruined by this louche man dressed in black, and his infernal left-wing racket! He just wouldn't leave her alone. After what had seemed like hours she had had enough, and sought out Bill to say goodbye, and to perhaps organise a date for them to meet without distraction. As she held on to this hopeful thought, she had found him kissing a giggling blonde girl with his hand inside her shirt, tickling her bellybutton. She left the party in a huff.

Like the relentless man who had put her in a bad mood that night, the midday sun pressed her down and made her feel helpless as she pushed her way through the dry yellow park. She could feel the sun eating away at her and she hated it. She felt like a spider put into a glass box and left in the sun to crumble and decay. She looked upwards toward the sun and sky. The clouds were bunched up and pompous, puffs of grey darkening against the white. Rain was coming. But when exactly was impossible to calculate. Sydney rain is capricious in nature. Just yesterday she had been walking home from the university and found herself caught in a shower. The schizophrenic types that spray down rain while the sun is shining so you can be simultaneously wet with rain and wet with sweat. This particular shower was more than usually dissonant because it had rained only on her side of the street. She looked across at a couple walking opposite; no rain at all. The street was split in two. One side clear and the other damp, hot and rainy.

What Hannah really pined for was a good heavy rain to gush over the city day and night and wash away the haze and sharpen up the world. Like the world was washed away and stripped clean every time she dived into the pool. But Sydney rain can't be relied upon, Hannah reflected. Hannah hated to be caught out on a day like this, bottled up in a box of heat, but she'd figured it should take her no longer than ten minutes to cut across the park to the shop, get her lunch, and hurry back home out of the haze. She walked quickly.

Ahead was a family playing on a swing set; two young boys on the monkey bars, a man with a grinning beard, and a woman shuffling around in a long black curtain. The long dark black seemed odd against the dull yellow day. Out of place and vulgar. Hannah felt her body hollow out, and a sleeping panic open its eyes in her stomach. The two young boys were hollering and yelling, swinging across the bars, happy as a birthday party. The grinning beard was a grinning and laughing. You could see that he was happy. The shuffling black curtain was shuffling around, but you couldn't see whether she was happy or not. Hannah almost felt like crying when suddenly the crescendo whine of a gardener's leaf blower consumed the park. The panic was now wide awake and alert, scratching against her teeth. She felt it when ugly men stared at her like dumb fish, she felt it when socialists waffled on about America and Israel, she felt it when the alternative types dressed in black flailed around in public like it was nothing to be ashamed of, and she felt it now as her eardrums were bludgeoned with the petulant whine of this infernal leaf-blower.

A leaf-blower starts with a growl, and then buzzes and whirs with indignation and self-righteousness until its amplified howitzer whine blankets the world. Like an ambulance hurtling down a city street. Loud and noisy and without any clear direction, it will scrub out everything, thought and reason, and bend the world to its mosquito scream. And once it starts there's no stopping it except for maybe a bomb in a beach bar or a ladies' nightclub, where 'all those slags are dancing around'. But even then you can never completely quell that mosquito whine. It will only retreat back into low growl: hurt, confused and vicious. Like a mediocre undergraduate with delusions of brilliance, receiving only a pass mark on his brilliant paper. Or a spoilt child refused candy, or a slack-jawed man staring at a computer screen. He'll retreat back to a growl until something new comes along. And there's always more leaves for a leaf-blower to blow away. Hannah really felt like crying. She was in the middle of the park now. She started breathing heavily. The haze was thick and heavy. It was heavier than she had anticipated. She knew that she could well be choked and mangled in this heat and sun and leaf-blower screech.

The buzz and whine crawled over her skin and breathed a hot, sticky whisper along her bones. The whine was very loud and powerful, and only getting louder. She tried to shake it off and hurry along, but it had taken over the park. Every point in space consumed by a hundred million mosquitoes, fat, satisfied and full of blood, pursing their lips, putting their hands on their hips, and squealing away like cornered pigs. She stopped suddenly and stood there in the middle of the park. She started to panic. The whole park was lit up with a pale drunk yellow. The bright colours of the park and swing set bled out by the lounging sun in the sky. Its soft breath cooing over Sydney and cooing over Hannah so that she felt every point in her body crawling with pain. Like a spider in a glass box left out in the burning sun to crumble and decay, minute by slow minute. She had to get out of the sun. She wanted to find some shade, and rest some. She scoured the park, her vision blurred as if refracted through burning diesel. No trees and no shade, only the yellow haze hanging over everything like a gas mask.

There was rain coming she knew, but when and where she couldn't tell because you can't bet on Sydney weather. There was no relief in sight. Standing in the middle of the park, her face wet with sweat and drawn tight in panic, she bent over and started to inhale more deeply. But the air didn't seem to satisfy. It was like breathing with thick gauze pulled over her mouth. She struggled to fill her lungs with air. What she needed was to go swimming. To plunge into a dark cavernous blue and annihilate the sun and the heat and the leaf-blower screech. Cocooned in dark blue all the high-pitched clanging of the world is brought down and made slow and deep, like listening to an erudite wise-man, or the rumbling of distant thunder.

Everyday before getting out and changing for class, Hannah would dip her head below the water line, close her eyes for a few seconds and feel the world brought under control. It blushed through her body and she felt free. Sometimes she would laugh with joy, her face underwater contorted in ecstasy. She felt the same sense of freedom dreaming about Bill in his red swimmers and in bed at night with a pillow between her legs. It was as if she could pull down thunder from the sky and put it between her thighs, and then let it rumble through her body so that her whole being would shake and tremble and explode into space.

In the park under the sun's canopy she felt like crying. Her body soaked with drunk heat and bent over, the gauze gas mask choking her, the sun eating into her, her face tight with panic. Like a spider in a glass box with millions of parched mosquitoes screaming at her and banging their fists against the glass, insane in their bewilderment. They could see her there, stilled, motionless and splayed out. All they had to do was smash the glass and then like a conveyor-belt, line up one by one to groan into her belly. Hannah really felt like crying so to stop herself making a scene, she straightened up, and walked quickly back home, away from the park and the heat and the leaf-blower screech.

Caitlin Still | # THE WATER

I
My mother says,
　　　I always thought
　　　That I would die
　　　By drowning

When we grew up,
We grew up swimming

In summer,
My dad liked
Putting seaweed on his head,
Sea monster-like

The Poseidon of this
Particular beach,
How he would laugh and roar
　　　Someone is coming
　　　To *get* you

Under the water,
My head runs quiet

II
When I was thirteen,
I fell in love with thoughts
Of death, and dying undersea,
　　　And swam,
　　　　　　Swam

Wistful-wise below,
I thought about
The process of drowning

It's not peaceful,
But long
And brutal

So I tried
To break the surface,
But gasped,
Saw lights

III

My family dies only
By natural causes,
But mother says,
        I know
        That I will drown

She told me of children
Who went to the ocean,
Who journeyed deep in the water,
And never came back

We were only
Very, very young,
And for years

They called to her, each night,
As she dreamt

Rafi Alam | PHILOSOPHER'S DRINKING GAME

Four philosophers walk into a bar,
And scrutinise their choices from afar.
Schopenhauer howls, 'I *Will* drink something light!'
A voice fusses: 'I Kant, I'm driving tonight.'
Back turned to the Abyss, did Nietzsche refuse?
While Hegel eventually settles between two.

Anastasia Kalos | CONCRETE BOX

Cate imagined two fiber-optic cameras tunnelling through her eyes. The two vulnerable yet memorable orbs prompted the eternal cliché about eyes serving as windows to the soul. It was as she pictured the camera tunnelling through her optic nerve that she considered the validity of the inner entity that her mother labelled a soul. The boxy public housing flat tainted Cate's thoughts; her mind had a fighting chance against the sedatives that reined galloping neurons. The brief holiday rudely ended at six in the morning, the time her mother's voice reached into Cate's sleepy mind like a backyard abortionist.

Larissa would yell repeatedly. *Wake up. Wake up. Wake up.* To add to Cate's annoyance, Larissa allowed an interval of one minute or thereabouts between shout outs. Perfectly timed, she thought. Shut up mother. The woman would wheeze some more as she shuffled to the bathroom, lugging the government provided metallic oxygen cylinder. Cate remembered the day her mother received the news. Doctor Banerjee offered the bad news first, thinking that the solution would soften the fact that her lungs had reached their use-by date. Banerjee shook his head as he spoke. *Emphysema, Mrs Petrova. No, no cure. But when it gets worse, you can always have oxygen.* He finished off with a toothy smile and passed her a Medicare slip to sign.

Cate's eyelids suddenly flicked open. The memory of the clunky oxygen cylinder rolling on the budget carpet floor like a military tank began to decay. If there was one thing that she appreciated, it was the way the cheap Department of Housing carpet muffled the passage of the tank. Ten years earlier, and the tank would have grated against polished concrete floor. Cate sat up and rubbed her eyes, dislodging crusty yellowish-green gunk. 'I'm up. I'm up,' she muttered.

Water continued running. Cate grumbled and pushed off her scratchy blanket. *Goddamn woman. Crone. Vampire.*

The stream slowed to the standard annoying series. Drip-drip-drip. The echo gained substance. It pounded against the door. Finding no welcome opening, it slid under the minute aperture between the door and carpet.

Cate's beseeching voice would inevitably pull her out of her slumber. 'Stop it! Just stop it, Mama. It's annoying. I'm tired. Stop running the tap!'

Drip-Drip …

'You never wake up. Wake up. I told you to wake up. The early bird gets the worm,' Larissa said, in Russian.

Must be a universal phrase, Cate thought. Her skin prickled beneath her blanket. *Who tucked in the blanket so tight?* She searched her memory, only to return empty. Each component rattled separately. The wretched water, its incessant sloshing against the basin. Brownish-red stains on thirty-year-old porcelain. When added together, the components presented a drab urban landscape.

If Cate could think of her life, sum it up like a convenient historic annotation, a large chunk of her existence blossoms in the concrete blocks that outsiders baptised 'suicide towers'. The logic behind the term related to the happiness factor or rather the lack thereof. Each time Cate braved her neighbours—the allegedly random assortment of drug addled single mothers, petty thieves and former convicts—she did her Christian duty; turning the other cheek, she would walk to the lift. As a child and teenager, she opted for the emergency fire stairs. Anything to avoid the vulgarities and name-calling. Her shortcuts ended after rumours spread about the as of yet unknown rapist who still surprised women. Cate suspected a long-term tenant.

She fought her blanket until she freed her arms.

'He has to be fifty or sixty now. Freak', she said.

Drip-drip-drip-drip.

'Jesus! Mum!'

Standing with renewed purpose, Cate shuffled to her bedroom door with intent only to question her capability of getting to the wretched bathroom to deal with the torturous sound. What a cubicle of a bathroom. Poorly fitted out, it made the colour beige look sexy. Customary to public design, the bathroom was close enough to smell—in Cate's mind—the cockroach shit and other detritus that made its way through pipes. Their government provided domicile, a haven for minorities (or 'wogs' according to her Anglo neighbours), junkies, ex-cons, the few single mothers receiving paid male company by day, thieves and pensioners. A social quick fix. Redolent of Sydney's oldest terrace house excavations at The Rocks, it represented the best and worst of social housing. Her mind failed to reach beyond her browbeaten psyche to rebuild the houses in her imagination. Each house was a hole in the ground that was surrounded by musty two-century-old stone that relayed the sadness and futility of early Sydney society. A portion of the residents within Cate's housing block struggled to get on. It didn't help that her building was named after James Cook. There on an illuminated awning, the explorer's name took precedence. When Cate read up on the illustrious Cook, she laughed at his demise. Hawaiian karma. As far as she was concerned her block, along with the other surrounding concrete housing estates, was modelled after its English predecessors. There was little chance of social improvement; children within the vicinity graduated from neglectful childhoods, attended disadvantaged public schools to be ejected into a life of physical and psychological ennui. Not all public housing children failed, but she had rarely encountered any success stories within her block. She thought, 'Here I am edging on 21 and looking forward to a key to nowhere.'

A niggling finger poked her from within. It poked with the sadistic tenacity of her former primary school deputy, Mr Chase. Cate didn't believe in déjà vu. Possibilities entailed a degree of fairness that was nowhere to be found within her concrete surroundings. A quick escape required personal upheaval. She would be reduced to an amnesiac, grasping for situations, memories and events to share with future acquaintances, friends and associates—those who were uncannily more fortunate during childhood. How else to move ahead or, according to the English, get on? Life was all about getting on, improving your lot, reducing the gap and finding a personal Elysian field, inner nirvana or small spot of privately owned land. You needed to strive against poverty and mediocrity. And you need not bother considering your neighbour, who was only trying to put out your eye in the process of getting ahead, moving up and beyond the steaming pile of urban overcrowding. *Oh mother, mother with all your peasant logic and blind prejudice. What are you to me but a millstone?*

Drip-drip-gurgle-glugggg-hssssss. The drip became a trickle.

Their arrival at the James Cook tenement, smack-bang in the decaying inner city of long ago was heralded by events beyond Cate's control. To Cate, destiny did not hover between the extremes of esoteric wonder and mystery. It attached itself to ordinary decisions and parental fuck ups, with children inheriting the repercussions of their parents' mistakes over time. Her parents divorced a year after her entry into the world. Her father returned to the loving arms of the motherland and a family that cried perennially, begging him to return to the home he belonged. Larissa's coworkers sympathised, assured her of her rights. It wasn't her fault, they said. It was her mother-in-law. Larissa kept her head down and worked hard at perfecting her stitching, constructing garments way before the clothing industry turned to China for manufacture. Larissa had spent her days sewing garments for the women who lived to arrange dinner parties, interior décor and their fanciful wardrobes. Each day, Larissa ran her fingers over the expensive fabrics and smiled, all the while thinking 'the wealthy sows will wear something that I, a lowly peasant, have touched first'. This perverse thought steadied Larissa's nerves as she ran seams and hems on her industrial Singer. It kept her mind even as she lit, what would be, a series of cigarettes on the sofa on her days off, watching midday variety shows and American soap operas. Larissa's cigarettes were 'her friends', so Cate could 'shut up and stop complaining'. Cate soon learned to give Larissa her personal space. A space that included mental quietude. No back chat. No talk. No complaints. Sure Cate thought, but Larissa would need her like all migrant parents need their children. Doctor Banerjee had explained as best as he could and Cate relayed his conclusions as 'emphysema, a degenerative disease of the lungs that would eventually require oxygen'. Then one afternoon, Larissa received delivery of the oxygen cylinder and her days as a machinist, putting together socialite garments, severed her association with Sydney's elite. Cate's sensitivity to her mother's alarming tetchy moods increased. It was back to the grey concrete surroundings and the blabbering television. This was before the reinvention of James Cook, before the addition of security intercoms that operated to allow authorised individuals in, such as the mailman who, before the advent of the internet, delivered hope in the form of catalogues and the occasional letter from faraway relatives, lovers and friends.

Cate gripped the round metallic doorknob and shut her eyes. She felt the icy metal chill caress her palm and inhaled in an attempt to focus and drown out the incessant aquatic echo. Drip-drip. Drip-drip-drip-shloosh. Shloosh-drip-drip. *It couldn't be. It shouldn't be.* And it wasn't. She turned the knob and pulled back fast enough to register a starburst of pain ripple through the big toe on her right foot. The impulse reached her brain like an icy fist that shook her foundations and up-ended thoughts that littered her brain like bric-a-brac dumped on nature strips. She stepped into the small hallway and eyed the closed bathroom door. It wasn't possible to hear the dripping water. Cate slammed the flat of her right palm against her ear like a swimmer bent on dislodging water, all the while thinking, *I have succumbed to a form of madness.* Her mind groped for answers. *Perhaps there was a dormant post-traumatic disorder that bypassed the guilt switch.* She looked at her feet to realise that she had slept in her singlet and underwear. Strangely enough her legs provided evidence of her winter fugue.

'I'm a forest. Hairy ape. Jesus' muttered Cate. She didn't subscribe to the radical feminist sector. She regularly shaved her legs though it was not due to any need to impress the opposite gender. It became a habit, a daily rite, except that her rites had slipped into a sinkhole. She turned the doorknob, but the gesture felt like six months had passed by between her waking and opening her bedroom door.

In the bathroom the porcelain basin remained dry. With held breath, she inspected the basin and exhaled until her head swirled. She gazed at her adversary in the mirror and pulled at her flesh. Her cheeks gave way, stretching easily enough between her thumb and forefinger. Her lips followed. She used the thumbs and forefingers in each hand as pincers and pulled her lower lip down and out. She repeated the gesture with her upper lip. Blinking rapidly, she sniffed the air and let go of her lips with a groan. The concrete walls caught hold of her primal sound and returned it at a lower volume. When it faded, leaving a slight tenderness in her vocal chords, Cate returned her gaze to the mirror and turned the cold water faucet with full force. Random drops splashed her neck. Cate scooped the water and slapped her cheeks vigorously. Each slap evoked questions relating to the return of her mother and the taps. There were no taps running the day she had returned from college and saw the body of her mother sprawled on the cold tiles. Stress impacted Larissa's routine existence: the fridge door was ajar, the balcony door remained half open, taps dripped constantly or at least until Cate returned home to chide her mother for being so forgetful. Only for her mother to shrug and say, 'The government pays for all the dripping water.' *Inconsiderate in life as in death.* One day Cate returned home, buoyant with pride and awe that she aced her mid-year exam, to discover the clothed body of her mother sprawled on the bathroom tiles and surrounded by the polite white boxes of tranquilisers, anti-depressants and paracetamol.

Cate covered most exit routes. Getting out of the mess that the media refashioned into the 'poverty trap' was as complicated as a Byzantine plot. There was the balcony, a quick route that would provide a once only experience in urban freefall. It was her mother's preferred exit, what was generally viewed —thanks to countless dramatic plots—as the easier option. Easy all right, Cate thought. Easy for those who heaved at the sight of blood. But dead was dead and the dead usually let go of their bodily functions. Some mornings Cate would hold her breath in her three minute showers, triggering her olfactory memory—if such a phenomenon existed. The environment could go to hell, she thought. The hypocrisy of it all. People purported to care for the environment yet turned a blind eye to the diseased social environments that government bureaucrats created for the have-nots. Even as Cate returned to *that* afternoon, she was unable to remember the order of events. It was a toss up between the eerie quietude and the acridity of shit and piss that whirled through the air like an ethereal swarm of wasps.

With fewer options to her, she decided to continue the lie. There were no financial benefits for bereaved teenagers, certainly not enough to enable self-sufficiency beyond public housing. Officials seldom cared about deaths. This was the decentralised society; so much information, yet too little time to check in on a dying or long-mummified neighbour. Larissa died during the afternoon on a weekday. The ambulance came and went without as much as a stir in the long housing commission hallway. All the neighbours were either out, working secret jobs, or minding their own business. Life carried on. The lie expanded, for the neighbours were ancient or well-versed enough in xenophobia to keep well away from the new Australians down the hall. Cate smiled until her cheeks ached. Then her right hand balled into a fist. She envisioned her fist through the small square of a government commissioned vanity mirror. Another potential escape. Each shard had a potential story to tell. Each story depended on a shard. The smaller pieces were ideal for cutters while the oblong pieces were for hardcore depressives seeking a final solution. No one got out of this life alive and no one could completely disappear. Everyone left a residue.

The world beyond urban poverty was focused on consuming the present and recycling past ideas. Cars, houses, accessories, gadgets, objets d'art, ten dollar internet porn, flirtation, haute cuisine, reality television, Nike, Louis Vuitton, Hermès, models, molecular gastronomy, the Beckhams, Prince William, celebrity gossip. Treadmills ran nonstop while Cate worked around the bitter tasting fog. If no-one cared enough to visit, she would refuse to care enough to inform the relevant bureaucracies. Weeks. Months. Five years and no-one questioned as long as the rent was paid. The electronic world of direct debits eradicated face-to-face interactions, further reducing the need for accountability and increasing public apathy. In the beginning, Cate amassed funds like an obsessive hoarder seeking a subconscious emotional high. On the fifth anniversary of her mother's death she ventured out and absorbed the futility within corporate offices and counted the dollars that propped up her pathetic salary as a corporate grunt. Bureaucracies preferred the bare minimum and orders. They worked as a unit, rarely collaborating with any other external department unless they were … ordered to. She looked in the mirror again and smiled. Noticing that her expression fell short of the Duchenne smile, she brought her eyes into the smile. Crinkle crinkle. Never mind the crow's feet. It would do, she thought. Yet the subtle odour hovered within the concrete vestibule. Five-year-old shit and piss with added foaming spittle that eerily reminded her of designer cuisine and the twenty-first-century foam garnishes of molecular gastronomy. Cate shivered with revulsion.

As she opened the vanity mirror, she saw medium sized scissors and added them to her shortlist of potential exits. A strategic gash in each wrist was sufficient, at least for those with irreversible emotional fatigue, whose daily mindset was like an extended version of the brief void that followed the sound of dying laughter. Cate reached for the scissors and assessed her reflection. Her hair, hanging way past her shoulders, pulled her face down. Each strand distorted all hope of a smile. No amount of straightening could shift the image of her mother. They had identical hair. Hair that hung like lead. Hair that weighed down their souls. Hardly the Old Testament stuff of Samsonite strength. Still, hair best represented a sanity of sorts. Crowning glories. Leonine manes. Clean versus greasy. Manageable versus the dreadlock roach motel sported by white Caucasian wannabes. It wasn't so much about the opinions of others rather than removing the weight in the same way a podiatrist excised a corn or a neurosurgeon removed brain tumors.

Cate began snipping. Each strand absorbed a variety of fumes, including Larissa's deathly effluvia. She began at the bottom, lopping off centimetre long chunks until she stepped into the Roaring Twenties with a Louis Brooks bob that blurted instant weight loss. Strands fell silently on the white porcelain. Done. Cate cocked her head from side to side, regarded her upgrade and inhaled deeply, depositing a light spray of vapour on the mirror. She gathered her hair clippings and deposited them in the small bin before running the tap to clear out the remainder of her previous self, the half panicked girl that woke from a distorted memory to enter the colder uncertainty beyond the confines of her mind, bedroom and flat. It was time to break through the emotional nefos.

Cate took one final look at her ensemble and made up face in the twenty dollar three-quarter mirror. Her new self gazed back and grinned. Laughter slid out with a smaller sliver of hope. Her laughter ricocheted off the concrete walls like a faux-thentic boomerang from Paddy's Markets. The moment trembled as her insides churned. She vowed to smile, nod and renegotiate; the laughter soon followed. Each raucous note mutated, unfurling like a butterfly emerging from its chrysalis until Cate merged with the altered persona. She gazed at her reflection. The animated individual within the silvery glass offered a synchronous grin, spoke of their urge to step out of the concrete box.

Cate nodded eagerly. 'And you will. You will. You really will.'

Tonya Westlake | SONNETS

I

Awakened, by soft silences at night;
the darkness whispers to me, echoed quests,
with faith, believe, I dance unto the light
for *credo quia impossibile est.*
I fear to wish upon a fading plight;
thus dashed upon the beach. To either side
I see great mountains obscuring the light
of drowned leaves; floating on the tide.

I lead myself through tireless tossing streams,
Azure to each horizon, endless; seems
lost among the screaming tides of dreams;
A hope of light from lie in speech was deemed.

I search alone through deep seas; coloured blue;
Those lost in washing waters; crushing truths.

II

A whisper to the wind in anguished pain,
of feelings doused in sympathetic hands.
To watch the ships sail; back from port again,
All searching for a once discovered land.

We're crushed against the corals'—bright red
A flash of 'fore known sailors set to seas.
Adorned in golden breeches; faithless; led
From safety; to impossibilities.

Disorder does move swift through waning light,
Relentless seas, attuned to form repent
Endangered; with no chance, no hope to fight,
Against the might of Truth's embodiment.

Forgetting not, that fear will never come,
To lead a tribe; your men, towards the sun.

III

A glimmer on the rocks obscures the light,
to feel in darkness, hope among the seeds.
A drizzle drives a petal into life,
Deep cravings, searching for an innate need.

To suffer at the hands of damning rain,

The glimmer fizzled out by flame dissolved;

Writhing, squirming, crying out in pain—
but in death, the petal glitters gold.

A peaceful mind, within my piece of mind
Detached through empty silences in air.
A movement begun deep, a movement blind
to the destination: a world, unfair.

In pain the world suffers, to fear the best,
as in a peaceful mind, pain lays to rest.

Connie Ye | # SCHOOLGIRL DRAMA

He weeps in the silence of the theatre,
Conscious spectacle, representative alien from another class.
They follow suit, one at a time,
Ragged mouths covered with curtain hands,
Propriety and sensibility, first order of the day.
(Let's watch anyway; so what if we don't understand?)
Which of them, if any, knows why he cries?
He belongs to morning mist
Reassured in the comfort of private feeling.
Who knows why *they* cry? Ill-suited, in general, to this sniffling sob Act,
The real story here is the two hundred girls infected, one way or another,
With varying degrees of desolation.

Matthew Withers |

PERPETUATING ABJECTION

WAR AND THE NARRATIVE OF SACRIFICE

If in some smothering dreams you too could pace
Behind the wagon that we flung him in,
And watch the white eyes writhing in his face,
His hanging face, like a devil's sick of sin;
If you could hear, at every jolt, the blood
Come gargling from the froth-corrupted lungs,
Obscene as cancer, bitter as the cud
Of vile, incurable sores on innocent tongues, —
My friend, you would not tell with such high zest
To children ardent for some desperate glory,
The old Lie: Dulce et decorum est
Pro patria mori.

> 'Dulce et decorum', Wilfred Owen

The news of Wilfred Owen's death reached his hometown of Oswestry, Shropshire on Armistice Day 1918, his mother ironically receiving the dreaded telegram to the backdrop of church bells gleefully extolling the arrival of peace. An embittered and vocal critic of the horrors of war in life, in death but another heroic soldier upholding 'the old lie': *dulce et decorum est pro patria mori*—'it is noble and glorious to die for your fatherland'.

The returned soldier is abject, his individual and social world decimated by the psychological and physiological terrors of warfare. Yet, paradoxically, the bodies of those who suffer most profoundly—the dead—become commodities utilised by the state to perpetuate such torment. Devoid of voice, their suffering is given meaning through nationalist narratives celebrating heroism and self-sacrifice in order to create a cumulative military legacy that endeavours to preserve the 'spirit of 1914'. Thus, the participation of future generations in wars of increasingly diminished purpose is ensured. This essay will examine how warfare as abjection impacted upon individuals and society in the First World War. It argues that veterans remained abject while the dead were glorified in order to construct the founding 'truth' of the modern military narrative, and that this rubric has been instrumental in legitimising subsequent political projects of war.

The 'spirit of 1914' refers to the enthusiasm that accompanied the outbreak of the First World War. While it primarily refers to the alleged jubilation of Germany, it is also used to express the optimism held by the allies. However this buoyant attitude quickly dissipated when it became clear that modern warfare had left no room for the 'military glory' of bygone eras.

As Omer Bartov remarked:

> The splendid bayonet charge over a field of flowers that so many soldiers had been taught to expect did not materialise. Instead, green fields were transformed into oceans of mud, frontal attacks ended up as massacres, great offences rapidly ground to a bloody halt, and heroic gestures were soon replaced by grim determination and a desperate will to survive.

And so stalemate occurred, trench warfare began, and soldiers found themselves living in what was effectively a dormant mass grave spanning 400 miles.

Enclosed in these squalid trenches, soldiers were entirely dislocated from normality. Their senses were relentlessly bombarded by the sights, sounds and smells of the Western Front—rotting corpses, rats, shells and excrement. The only normative connection the soldier had to his world was the unobscured sky above, which in itself connoted exposure to the ever-present threat of shelling. Consequently the soldier faced constant abjection; his world collapsed and was replaced by the persistent threat of death, which even if not realised, was still likely to produce physical and mental damage. In this case the implications of war as abjection on the individual world are clear. If the soldier was not killed he was severed from his world and scarred by the experience of constantly confronting the materiality of his existence. The social implications of this abjection are complex and implicitly entwined with the political project of war, as suggested by the experiences of Owen's friend and fellow war poet, Siegfried Sassoon.

At the end of a period of convalescent leave in 1917, Sassoon, who held strong anti-war sentiments despite being a decorated soldier, refused to return to duty, instead writing a letter to his commanding officer entitled 'Finished with the war: a soldier's declaration'. The declaration was subsequently read out in parliament. Rather than court-martial a decorated soldier, the government declared Sassoon unfit for service and issued treatment for neurasthenia or 'shell shock'. This demonstrates both the government's preference of sidelining Sassoon as mentally unstable over discrediting an archetypal soldier who fitted their military narrative. Statistical analysis conducted during the early years of the First World War indicated that over ninety per cent of patients were returned to duty in a short period of time, frequently worsening their condition. Furthermore, the British government did not perceive physically disabled servicemen to be the state's responsibility—'disabled ex-servicemen ... were entitled only to a gratuity in respect to their injury; the state was not obliged to ensure the man's reintegration into society'. Consequently, when soldiers returned home, the abjection caused by war often imposed upon their social worlds. The outspoken were often ostracised, the psychologically scarred left insufficiently treated and the physically disabled neglected.

Ironically, while the survivors of war were stripped of their significance, the corpses of the fallen had meaning bestowed upon them.

Regardless of his opinions in life, the soldier, once dead, becomes a commodity of the state. The state acts as a mouthpiece for corpses unable to communicate, funnelling the tragic and horrific demise of a whole generation into a single narrative of sacrifice to lie as the cornerstone of a new military legacy. In this manner the active revulsion and disillusionment of soldiers like Owen is nullified, his body usurped by the state's political project to aid that which the soldier so detests; 'only alive did he sing: that is, only alive ... did he determine the ideas and beliefs that would be substantiated by his own embodied person and presence'. With modern warfare having completely extinguished the romantic notion of war, a substitute narrative was needed to make meaning of suffering, and the concept of sacrifice filled this role. Given the magnitude of fatalities in modern warfare, military rhetoric largely avoids the discussion of death. However, as Neal Curtis notes, 'when death is recorded ... it is invariably a key moment in the sublimation of violence as heroic sacrifice'. Consequently, the mass of corpses produced by the First World War came to signify not fear and abject suffering, but the nobility of heroically sacrificing one's life for one's country. And so 'the war to end all wars' became 'the war to incite all others'.

In almost every Western war since the First World War the narrative of sacrifice has been called upon, and with each new episode of suffering it is developed further, creating a cumulative military legacy stretching from the 'spirit of 1914' to the current war in Iraq. The 'spirit of 1914' bears importance as it represents the pinnacle of popular enthusiasm to fight for one's country: 'the relationship between the risking of life and the movement of spirit, a central motif in the rhetoric of warfare, was nowhere more striking (or tragic) than in the enthusiasm that met the outbreak of the First World War'. This was undoubtedly due to the fact that during nearly all stages of the First World War, there was a genuine underlying threat to sovereignty among the European powers, a feature of war that has been largely absent in the Western military conflicts which followed the Second World War. However this cumulative military legacy allows the political project of war to continue its false application of the original narrative of sacrifice to give meaning to corpses produced by wars of diminished purpose. Therefore the soldiers killed and made abject for ideological reasons in Vietnam, for colonial reasons in the Falklands and for economic reasons in the current war in Iraq, are still understood to be making a heroic sacrifice for their country. This is a grotesque new chapter of 'the old lie' that so plagued Owen.

Warfare as abjection destroys both the individual and the social worlds. It strips the individual of all normative references and subjects them to horror hitherto unimaginable. The ubiquity of death, a constant reminder of the materiality of self, almost invariably drives the individual into the abyss of abject suffering. This suffering continues when veterans find themselves unable to reintegrate into society, often ostracised by various disabilities and beliefs. Yet most tragic is not the individual suffering, but the countless repetition of its occurrence as a result of the Western narrative of sacrifice, distilled from the 'spirit of 1914' and bolstered by the countless dead since. By continually tapping into these nationalist narratives through a cumulative military legacy, the meanings of wars have falsely converged to benefit the political project of war. The same sentiments of self-sacrifice and national duty that were espoused by an endangered sovereignty in the First World War and retained through the narrative of sacrifice are still accessible to governments waging war for less important issues of national interest today. Accordingly, warfare as abjection will inevitably continue to destroy the individual and social worlds of future generations, their corpses proof of suffering, given meaning through a fallacious notion of sacrifice.

References

Bartov O (2000). *Mirrors of destruction: war, genocide, and modern identity.* New York: Oxford University Press.

Cohen D (2001). *The war come home.* Los Angeles: California University Press.

Curtis N (2006). *War and social theory: world, value and identity.* New York: Palgrave Macmillan.

Fussell P (1975). *The Great War and modern memory.* London: Oxford University Press.

Hart-Davis R (2004). Sassoon, Siegfried Loraine (1886–1967). In *Oxford dictionary of national biography*, Oxford University Press [Online]. Available: www.oxforddnb.com/view/article/35953 [Accessed 31 May 2011].

Jones E & Wessely S (2001). Psychiatric battle casualties: an intra- and inter-war comparison. *British Journal of Psychiatry,* 178(3): 242–47.

Scarry E (1987). *The body in pain: the making and unmaking of the world.* Oxford: Oxford University Press.

Verhey J (2000). *The spirit of 1914: militarism, myth and mobilization in Germany.* New York: Cambridge University Press.

Jonathan Payne | MUSE
WHISPERS

Roots evolving lie dormant, beneath those sleeping orbs.

Moisture swallows, yawning breathless,
Under the surface, the shell floats seemingly still,
Out of breath, stifled—
Though calm, enveloped in earth, all encompassing bosom,
Blossom and the shadow texture of its embrace.

Beneath consciousness, above,
All colours of perception are revealed.
Digging into experience they act,
Animating flesh.

So much forgotten and revealed.
This, for all eternity muse whispers,
An interrelational secretive space.

Scorching heat dries, dissipating the skin, leaving only
Rock and sand,
The stagnant and bereft.
Moisture.
Liquid flows out from below, hinted texture upon seething bleak infinitude.
First: clear, translucent. It soon turns a deep dark red.
Rich and sickly sweet.
Gentle and nourishing, it urges ever—
Remember: the end, the wasteland.

Parallel, with ashen texture, a mass of flesh expounds, urges, pollinating, transgressing and destroying, enveloping evermore. Departing, leaving only shell. Leaving growth, decay.

Mulch, growing, twisting, tangled mass. The undergrowth finds its careful way,
Sits forever, strangling the Earth.

Earthworms feast as the garden breaks down.
Forever and over, forever again.
The soil beneath earth above bears gifts ripe for new growth.
Creation borne upon backs broken, feigned joy amid the morbid erotic.
Release,
Departing.

At once reborn and eternally changed,
New flesh connects to all that has come before: the path, the garden, deep dark red, ocean abyss.

Andrew James Milne | # FOLLOW ME DOWN

Follow me down
Remove yourself from that town
Turn inward
Turn outward
I am on my last go around

Identifying the difference
I get lost in the darkness
Of the deep waters,
Surround me
Now I only must confess
Of a desirable caress

To steer this train wreck
From impending doom
Like walking a horse
To the waters
Of a consecrated room

Stooped in symbols
And confounded by a medium
That constricts and controls
I choose to relate
The heavy tolls of my psychotic break

Not a breakdown
Only a breakthrough

I went to the other side, cut off my hands
And now don't have to
Live up to anything holding true

My energy runs along my veins
But it spurts out in bloody red stains
Splashed and splattered all over a page
Dye that hopefully won't hurt anyone's name
Only bound to my own mind made cage

Can you feel the life that courses our veins?
Do you breathe the life that flows in our names?
Beyond the name and beyond the blood
I know it hurts, we all feel its hurt
We all feel its love; we all see its game

Its simple suppleness
Its unruliness
Taught to be controlled
Lived to let live
To be an everlasting unfold

Andrew James Milne | # MADNESS IN THE NIGHT SKY

When I look into the night sky
The moon and stars beckon recovery
A long-lost love that passes by
Like looking into them as a child
In innocent amused contemplation
Of the vast nothingness in observation

All that lies beyond
What can and can't be known
Fascinated by this infinite pond
You and I stare away
Yet can't help but part and fray

When I look into your eyes
I see a curved crescent
They sparkle like the dull city skies
Those muted tones fall into a descent
If only I could see true reflection
Across the sunbathed Sahara
In a vastly clear sunrise

To the depths of my emotions
I swam to the bottom of those oceans
To find nothing but myself
Naked and free to be lost
Away from your judging gaze
But terribly confided to the mind's maze

Like a cavernous mountain in the Himalayas
I yearned for my place of solitude and isolation
I saw a black snake and heard the drumming of sticks
Wanted to sit in perfected elation
Yet got lost in gulps of saltwater
As my mind was not freed but ripped

My body a machine of energy
I danced the mad man's dance
Spaced into a trance
I was soon not able to see
And failed to seize my chance

Deluded with the fear of death
Just let me jack my dick before I go
One last sensation before I slipped
Deep down into unconsciousness
Fighting my saviours
I was held down and sedated

Pricked and pinned I tore out my drip
Smeared blood on the wall,
Ran the halls naked announcing that I could fly,
That I was never going to die
I climbed my hospital bed like it was a cliff
Trying to escape my demise
I ran barefoot looking for your eyes
Attempted to hitch a ride to the west
And just go sleep and get some real rest

To see my long-lost love
And reclaim my own heart

———

Drugged continuously I wandered
The halls like a zombie
I wish they would have left me be

Moon and sun return to me
Give me back my normal life
To come back to the reality of this city
And put my paranoia and anxiety to rest
Please pull out this wretched knife.

Jessica Regan | TRAPPED IN THE NET

He opened his eyes and white light assaulted him. Lifting a heavy hand to shade his face, he sat up and fought off a wave of dizziness. Suppressing the urge to vomit, he tried to look around himself. Everything was light blue, fading into white above.

From a distance, he heard a bird singing. He turned his head, trying to find a source for the sound, and realised it was coming from directly above him. A small, blue bird was hovering near the top of his head. It fluttered down and landed on his knee, looking at him curiously. It tweeted, and he understood it.

'Hello.'

Confused, he answered with the first thing that came to mind.
'Hi. You're a bird.'

'I know that. You are not meant to be here.'

It had a light, lilting voice. A voice that one would have expected from a bird. A talking bird, not a tweeting one. Okay, there was something wrong with that.

'Birds aren't supposed to talk. What the hell? Where am I?'

'Can you please leave? I have a lot to handle at the moment.'

'A lot to handle? The place looks empty to me. I'd like to know why I'm here. And why I'm talking to a bird. Why is everything blue? I thought—'

'You ask too many questions.'

'What the hell? I just got cut off there. That was really weird. It was like I just couldn't say any more words at the one time. Do you know—'

'Look, they're going to start soon. Personal problems, irrelevant information, opinions I don't care about, even bodily functions.'

'What are you talking about? I'm worried here. I might have some weird kind of speech defect. And who is going to start soon? I really don't—'

'Really, I don't know who actually reads half their bullshit. It seemed like a good idea at the time, but I'm tired of it now.'

'It happened again! What is wrong with me?'

'Oh. Yes, you. Shit. Um, it's hard to explain to people who haven't done it before. You can't speak using more than 140 characters at a time.'

'Why? What's the point?'

'It's just how it works, okay? Part of the novelty. Microblog or something. Can you leave now? There's a lot of … Oh god, they're coming.' #panic

This bird started flitting about irrationally. Panicked, like it needed to escape, it tried to fly up and down, but ended up just flying in tight circles. He supposed it had gone crazy. He couldn't see anything for miles. Everything was still just a clear, light blue.

He stood up shakily. A small line of text appeared from nowhere and floated close to his face. It read, 'I'm hungry.' As soon as he read it, it froze, and held its position in the air.

He turned around and another small line of text appeared. This time it had @barackobama at the beginning and said 'My mum says please increase her social security checks. She thanks you in advance.' Hold on, he thought. Was this a message to Barack Obama? *President* Barack Obama? How could anyone just contact him so casually like this?

The sentence then duplicated itself. Instead this time it had the letters RT in front of it. 'RT?'

'Re-tweet,' tweeted the bird. 'You like something someone tweets, you re-tweet it. That way all your followers can see it too.'

'Followers?'

'Now, if you insist on being here, just stay out of the way.' #annoyed

'Wait, there are other people here? Are people *following* me?' #panic

'Well of course, otherwise, what would be the point of saying anything?'

'And they're *listening* to me?'

'They can hear everything you're saying, but no one is really listening. No one ever really listens.'

'Well, then what is the point of saying anything?'

The bird remained silent, cocked its head at him for a moment and flew away.

The words gradually began to build up around him, frozen in different places in space. He saw a cluster of tweets, that all had something in common. They all had a hashtag in front of them. In one cluster, the hashtag was followed by 'ineedtostop'. Intrigued, he read a few.

#ineedtostop texting you if you still tYp3 lIk3 DiHzz

#ineedtostop stalking @justinbieber because I know he'll never notice me :'(

#ineedtostop Procrastinating! My schoolwork is piling up and my grades are going down.

'What does the hashtag mean?' he asked, still reading.

'You do it to tag something. Like a topic you're talking about, or an emotion, or anything really. Must be trending.'

'Trending?'

'Urgh, you really are a noob. When a lot of people are talking about one thing at the same time, that thing is trending.'

'That's neat, I guess ... so if something happens, and everyone is taking about it, then it trends?'

'Now you're getting it :)'

'Hey, and I'm getting used to this 140 character thing!' #yay

There were tweets from famous people trying vainly to get in touch with their fans, or at least prove to them that they were normal human beings. There were world leaders, pointlessly trying to contact uncaring voters. But mostly, there was an overwhelming amount of normal, boring, average people. They were trying to be 'individual', trying to show their 'unique' personality to no one that cared.

He began to grow bored of reading them all.

He reached out to touch one of the small lines of text, but his hand just moved through it. He looked down at his fingers. They were black and wet, as if he had just touched ink.

The tweets slowly began to turn the blue around him black. They twisted and curled around both him and the bird. Soon he couldn't move without touching them, his clothes began to get soaked, and his face was covered in black droplets. The bird was becoming more and more panicked. It soon became apparent that it was too much. The bird was too small; it couldn't handle this onslaught of pointless information.

The bird stopped. It dropped out of the air, landing in his hands. Its tiny chest pulsed up and down, and he could only see the whites of its tiny eyes.

The words melted and fell to the ground like rain. The tweets kept coming, but they instantly turned to liquid, so the black rain didn't stop.

Suddenly he was underwater. He couldn't breathe. Holding tightly onto the bird, he thrashed his legs and arms, trying to swim upwards. He broke the surface of the water and gulped in air. The bird was still unconscious, and he held it above water, hoping it was alive.

The water behind him surged. He tried to swim away as rapidly as he could while still holding the weak, tiny bird. A giant whale rose up out of the water beside him. Its pupil dilated as it saw his tiny bobbing figure in the water.

The whale seemed to smile, then spoke.

'Hi, I'm the fail whale.'

The whale opened its mouth, and the tide of tweets flowed in, including him and the bird. He could do nothing as its giant mouth slowly closed, and he saw the line of blue light slowly disappear into blackness.

He blinked a couple times, and realised his computer screen had gone blank. He rubbed his face and reached over to move the mouse. The screen lit up, and the bright, light blue background almost blinded him. The image of a smiling whale, being carried by eight small birds dominated his screen. 'Twitter is over capacity.' What a waste of time.

Frustrated, he clicked the Facebook tab.

Jordan Roe | # THREE POEMS FROM A FOX TO AN OTTER

I—Geblissung

You crept nearer, tide-like, sluicing
On my parched sandstone shore, we played.
Your tickling trickles salved and caressed
My silted bank, your waves suffusing.

Wandering warping chords found blithe
Reception as they soared over
Sliding voices with billowing starts—
Our windborne glee! Salty and lithe.

You swell and you glisten to
Day's binding tempo,
Forgetting stillness, spraying out,
Elatedly falling beyond view.

—

Fallen all over me, streamed
Down to draw, telling lines,
My cascading wrinkles, lovelorn creeks
And laughter splashed, monsoons dreamed.

A magnetic embrace, we form
Yang and Yin, you channel within

So perfectly quenching, I crumble
And drift through your storm.

And with this togetherness all
Past's half tragic treasures
With th'ideal morrow awaken
To presently, simply, befall.

II—Aubade

Wake please and please and glow your golden smile,
The sun does his and the Angelus chimes.
Through rousing streets rolling: a wandering howl
Their legendary louré of ambling time.
But on your still face those rambling hours
Stay gorgeously stagnant like summer-baked flowers.

III—Ode

Walks 'round the town, cones 'round the clock
Mischief and cheek resound and glow.
Through lacy terraced vistas flow
Meandering routes recount their days
Bearing nights, weary and epic,
Time turbulent and dynamic

Like a pair of owls glide on dawn's zephyr,
Home from thrilling moonlit bouts,
We coasted harmony,
The lust remote.

So when you soared wayward off with whim,
I was seared with tears of lurid fathoming.

I cupped your opal jaw and grimaced
For though it glistened
Its fleetingness, I realised,
Was sickening.
Your uncaring brow, and on your lips I see
A removed smile, you couldn't help me.

Soothing, these discrete presentiments
Found while swaying with air's uproar;
I saw a deep gully's furl,
Followed its breath,
Through a leafy gap, to forest's cobalt haze,
A dome of dreamlike revelled lust.

Nicholas John Margan | # THE MASK (EXCERPT)

The fish within David's eyes swam happily in circles at the sight, his lips peeled back to frame his crooked smiling teeth. The focus of the peoples changed from him to those around, to the lights of smiled hellos long left hidden. He climbed his way to land his feet back upon the ground, the light of the shining stones licking up upon his feet and the air circling his still flailing limbs. He stood for a moment, 'TAP TAP', the smile still upon his lips. Then, with a head that circled about the radiant glow of the awakened night, from star to star and street to street he limb-fluttered, left right left left, his way to the exit of the town. With one last look at the glow that stood shocked from out of the depths where it had been hidden, he followed the path back home. Each lamp that had lit upon the sound of his walking feet before, faded slowly back to sleep, the path behind fading into nothingness, not dark but hidden once again. At last upon his doorway he stood, the house still leaning thin and crooked out upon him, out to welcome him from the sea of which he was a ship come tired home. He entered, falling into the arms of the green velvet dark wood chair. His window eyelids closed upon the fish that slowed to stop quite sudden and a cloak of deep and peaceful sleep softened the light by which they swum.

Dominic Mcneil | # FLYING SHIPS AND TURNING TIDES

The diversity of languages in which works of literature may be written, seemingly presents an impenetrable barrier for the reader of one language to interpret the text of another. Yet the ability to translate provides not just a means to grasp the meaning of a linguistically foreign work, but it also provides a testimony to the commonality of all languages—the fact that they can be so readily translated proves that they are both tokens[1] and facilitators of human thought. With this in mind, we are not so much translating phonemes and words, clauses and sentences as we are interpreting structure and metaphor from one medium into another, and through this, understanding the themes of a work and hence the thought that has gone into it. The difficulty in translating a work such as *Beowulf* lies not so much in the language barrier—which in itself is considerable— but rather in the obstruction which is understanding the thoughts of a people separated from us by more than a thousand years, and the radically changed world that has developed during this time. The short passage of a mere nineteen lines (lines 210–228) provides a remarkably deep insight into the character of the medieval Germanic peoples, and it is from translations and subsequent interpretations of their literature that we may continue to understand one of the forerunners to our current world.

---

1 Token: the materialisation of a given type: e.g. the book (token) and the novel (type)—hence language (token) and human thought (type). NB: tokens may change into the forms of different languages e.g.: French and English are all tokens of the same type—human thought.

The basic structure of the passage operates around the principles of repetition and recurrence, with the text appearing in pairs. The very first half-line of the passage: 'Fyrst forð gewat'[2] recurs in the precise midpoint of the passage with the reference to an approaching time: 'oðþæt ymb an-tid'.[3] In this way, the passage is effectively divided into two halves, with each being heralded by the coming of a specified time. Therefore the structure of the passage highlights both the passing of time, and the prefiguration of events. In general, this pattern features prominently in the passage, with the opening depiction of the 'flota ... on yðum'[4] and more importantly, the boat being moored under cliffs: 'bat under beorge',[5] an image which is found in the third last line: 'sæ-wudu sældon'.[6] This focus on an anchored ship is accompanied by a second focal point of the passage, namely the depiction of armour being brought onto and off the ship as 'secgas bæron ... beorhte frætwe'[7] and the later, 'syrcan hrysedon, guð-gewædo'.[8]

These two structural components which frame the extract around ships and armour relate to some of the overall themes in the passage. In effect, the depiction of the moored ship reinforces the maritime nature of the Germanic peoples. This societal facet is further seen in the general thematic development of the passage, such as the multiple depictions of maritime scenery with the marine terminology of the 'sund wið sande',[9] 'brim-clifu blican'[10] and 'side sæ-næssas'.[11] In addition to this are the depictions of cliffs: 'beorgas steape'[12] and the 'beorge' in the opening sentence.

---

2 'The time departed forth' (line 210a)
3 'until about a time' (line 219a)
4 'the ship ... on the waves' (line 210b)
5 'a boat under the hill' (line 210a)
6 'the wooden sea-[vessel] moored' (line 226a)
7 'the warriors bore ... bright ornaments' (lines 213b, 214b)
8 'mail shirts and battle-clothing rattled' (lines 226b–227a)
9 'sea against the sand' (line 213a)
10 'shining sea-cliffs' (line 222a)
11 'wide sea-headlands' (line 223a)
12 'steep hills' (line 222b)

Furthermore, the poet chooses to devote a sizeable amount of the passage to the depiction of the sea itself with the inclusion of various words for waves: 'yðum' (line 210b) and 'wæg-holm' (line 217a) as well as the use of the word 'streamas'[13] to indicate the tide and 'sund'[14] to denote the ocean. Finally, in reinforcing this maritime constituent of Germanic culture, the poet suitably refers to the Weders as 'liðende'[15] thus cementing their status as a seafaring people. Likewise, the passage as structured around the bearing of armour emphasises the adventurous and at times bellicose nature of the Germanic peoples. This is reinforced by the occurrence and recurrence of a vocabulary which evokes the eagerness of the warriors and their desire for adventure. The crossing of the sea is described by the compound noun 'wil-sið' (line 216a)—the desired-journey—whilst the Geats themselves are depicted as 'Beornas gearwe' (line 211b)—the ready warriors. Furthermore, the boat itself is 'winde gefysed' (line 217b)—hastened by the wind—in an evocation of the Germanic eagerness for adventure, a cultural facet mirrored in the way that the Weders 'hraðe ... on wang stigon'.[16] Evidently the passage is structured in concord with the development of these themes, namely the maritime and adventurous nature of the Germanic peoples.

Another important linguistic feature to consider in understanding this passage, and in general all literature, is the use of metaphor. This passage from *Beowulf* presents three important metaphors that need to be analysed. Firstly, the half-line, 'streamas wundon'[17] evokes the turning of the tide and thus in the tradition of Old English literature, serves as a metaphor for a concurrent change in fortune. The tide comes, symbolising the departure of the Geats, the beginning of the journey, and with this the changing of the waters prefigures the changing in fortune. This change in fortune can be reasonably inferred to be the beginning of the end of

---

13 'streams' (line 212b)
14 'sea' (lines 213a, 223b)
15 'seafarers/sailors' (line 221)
16 'quickly climbed onto the plain' (lines 224b–225)
17 'the streams rolled' (line 212b)

Hrothgar's troubles, a change which Beowulf's coming is responsible for. Consequently the use of metaphor not only aids the narrative as a form of prefiguration, but it also communicates the thematic idea of prophecy and the ordering of the future. The second metaphor is evident when the ship of the Geats is anthropomorphised into human form through the use of the term 'bearm'[18] to describe the hull of the ship. By describing the ship as a living entity, the poet illustrates the importance and centrality of the ship to Germanic culture, especially to the North Germanic peoples whose coastal and insular geography can account for this. This observation is reinforced by such discoveries as the Sutton Hoo burial, whereby the sanctity of the ship is demonstrated in its application as a burial vessel for the highest orders of society. Finally the ship undergoes a second metamorphism in its transformation into a bird through the metaphor, 'flota fami-heals, fugle gelicost'.[19] In becoming a bird, the ship accords to a deep-rooted English literary convention whereby birds are used as motifs, caricatures and anthropomorphic embodiments of meaning. This literary feature is extensive in Old English works, with the swan, gannet, curlew, seagull, eagle, tern and cuckoo all featuring prominently in the elegy The Seafarer whilst the phoenix is present in the poem of the same title. By considering the anthropomorphism of the ship into a bird in the context of all English literature, the metaphor can be seen to evoke a transcendence in the form of freedom—the freedom one experiences by being separated from society on the landless ocean. Curiously, the poet selects the verb 'gewaden'[20] to describe the passage of the ship through the water—a verb which can be translated as trudged, and is also the source of the Modern English derivative 'waded'—which seems to go against the earlier depiction of the ship as a bird. Nevertheless this metaphor is extended to the warriors themselves, who after disembarking from the ship shake their armour: 'syrcan hrysedon, guð-gewædo'[21] as a bird shakes

---

18 'bosom' (line 214)
19 'the foamy necked boat most like a bird' (line 218)
20 'trudged' (line 220)
21 'mailshirts and battle-clothing rattled' (lines 226b–227a)

its feathers. Thus, not only is the ship free on the open water, but also the warriors who are carried by it.

In conclusion, the structure, thematic development, use of metaphor and at times the specific use of words are all crucial and interrelated to the exposition of meaning in the aforesaid passage as they provide the reader with a vivid display of Germanic culture. In translating such works, it is crucial that one prioritises maintaining the semantics of the passage over the secondary considerations of phonological, syntactic and etymological similarity between original and translation. This illustration of culture involves but is not limited to, the symbolism of the waves and tides of the ocean as change and fortune, the utility of the bird as a metaphor and caricature, and the coming together of these two in the depiction of the living ship as a focal point of Germanic culture. In illuminating societal traits as well as cultural literary conventions, this extract from Beowulf provides an insight into Anglo-Saxon thought and literature, and most importantly, the society in which it was created.

References

Original Old English text taken from:
Alexander M (Ed)(2000). *Beowulf: a glossed text.* London: Penguin Books.

Translation aided by the lexicon of:
Mitchell B & Robinson FC (Eds)(2007). *A guide to Old English.* Seventh edn. Oxford: Blackwell Publishing.

Robert Ribbons | FAIRYTALE

Underneath the sweetness
The house reeks of rot
She watches secretly
Scours her bleeding cunt
Orgasms
Fondles the scent
Of their uncooked flesh.

The children lick
With their purple tongues
Teeth black
From chewing licorice
They gobble, they grunt,
They gorge on gingerbread
Their insatiable fingers
Clawing through sugar
And dread.

Tom Gooch | # WELCOME TO MICHIGAN

GREAT LAKES, GREAT TIMES

Detroit, MI

Do you know the way the light folds and flickers off a gentle harbour before its rays sulk off into the cool purple depths of night? I don't. How could I? I've never left Detroit. I almost left the county once, on a school excursion, but I don't know if that counts as travel.

My brother's been all over the place—even the south-west. He told me that there were girls down there that would breathe alcoholic vapours into your mouth as the hot night sweated around you and then they would push you away and walk off as quickly as they had appeared. A place where a foreign needle plunged into your arm and you ran around like a lone cub without its pack in the cold alpine mountains of dust. I didn't really believe him though. He probably just read that somewhere—or maybe I did.

Mom and my father only heard about the grades and the job he was offered at the end of it all. His fucking job.

—That's great John! That's great, they said.

I waited for the 'We're proud of you son.' It came. In equal parts clichéd and unfamiliar. My father was genuinely buoyant that night:

—At least you won't have to slug it out in the yard like I've had to. Pissing away my years managing these little pricks that don't even want to be there. You can get into proper management.

He looked down seriously at the dry lamb chops and boiled peas that were spread across his plate.

–

The Scholarship Examination

I turned over the crisp white page.

'Write a creative piece detailing a spiritual or cultural experience that has been highly influential in determining the person you are today.'

I looked over at the other students. A girl feverishly scribbling about an exotic land. A spiritual epiphany that I had never had.

I tried to write about hockey. I cringed. There was some culture to it. You could say that it binds us here. Men who played as boys in frozen puddles, and screamed and knocked and struck as the dark fell on abandoned car parks. I tried to remember the feeling of my hands on the stick but I'd forgotten. All I could remember was my hands fumbling over latches at the docks or the feeling of the goalie glove on my cold hand when my father was coaching John.

Could I write about how that didn't work out? That doesn't really answer the question. Business schools want success stories. So I lie.

–

Great Expectations

My brother entered the room. Quiet. Guarded. He was so confident most of the time.

—How was it?

I looked at him.

—I didn't know what to write. I had to lie.

—For the story? It's fiction. Not real. Isn't fiction always a lie?

—I don't know.

—You'll get in. You're a smart kid. You're going to make a lot of money.

I paused.

—The Red Wings are playing Saturday, I said. Against Pittsburgh. Want to go?

—I think I'll have work. Sorry bro.

—You said that last time.

—I had work last time too. Man's gotta work.

—You sound like—

—Don't.

—But you do.

—I sound like anyone who has worked on those fucking docks and wanted something better.

—You sure got something better. You know you could have played.

—I was injured.

He went out to the window to look outside. A dark violet sky.

—I'll let you know about Saturday.

He walked out.

—

Dissent

I have received two letters from Columbia University in my life. They were both last summer.

Letter one: 'I am writing to you to congratulate you on your acceptance into the 2011 Scholarship Program at The Columbia University School of Business.'

Summer that year was promiscuous. It hinted, hid, dwindled, sprawled, flew and eventually left. In Fall, the weatherman said that it was as if it had never come at all.

Letter two: 'Thank you for your correspondence. Whilst your indefinite deferral forfeits your status as a university student for next year, previous acceptance to the School of Business will be counted in your favour, should you decide to re-apply in the future. Kind regards.'

Denver, CO

And so I left. Now I load freights in Denver. The winter still numbs me. In our breaks I sit with the older men on frozen steel girders staring out over the yard into the endless and eternal white. A greying man of sixty turns to me. I ask him why he works here. What led him to come here. He says that sometimes our dreams burn so quickly that they soon fall and are gone. He bravely draws on a cigarette before throwing it out into the snow as it cools and the light of the tobacco goes out and soon ceases to exist at all.

Michela Ziady | COPYWRITER

giddy girl jumps at j-
ob in big firm to play
ticklish tricks
with wrig
                    gly
            words

in the playground's office, Cadillacs drive through ceilings
patent leather sofas soak up jackets, junk and YouTube and MeTube noise
posters and gimmicks mimic our culture of cool because the creative
process always begins in
the doorway framed with hipster vinyls
and mashable-trashables.

(remember, the consumer is Your Wife.)

smarty pants, stay in the agency of Eden and try—hard—to create
Big Ideas for beaten brands.
eve's apples don't go crrrrunch.

'great ads' = only the right copy. so stick
2 the > because then, you will

            see
                        your
            digital
                        Name

in

                              pixelated

skies.

                        Giddy!

But forever after, in the land of
spin and squeeze, keep the art
from your vein not the same
as anyone (or Evron) else.

Elizabeth Goralewski | # GUMMO
GET GROUNDED

'What shit did you tell them, you black prick?' The green gummy bear tightened his grip on the liquorice strip, and forced his blade into the skinny laxative's neck—head—shoulder—whatever. The whole clan of liquorice had sold them out to the Fruits, causing all out war in Mund City, and regardless of what he said right then, however closer he got Gummo to the Enjoyment Orb, he was going to end up losing the top quarter of his form. Paring knife or not, that blade was good enough to damage any kind of Fruit ally.

The strip quivered in his grip, twiggy arms rattling the cuffs at the wrists.

'I didn't tell them anything, I swear! It was all Lionel! He's the head of our group! I'm just a helper monkey! I'm still learning—' A phone rang in Gummo's pocket.

'What?'

'Gummo! We got Lionel! He's the head honcho of this bastardy!'

'I know,' he growled into the phone. 'I just got that out of one of his minions.' He hung up.

He pushed the liquorice into the wall as hard as he could. 'Don't squirm,' he growled, and proceeded to hack ferociously through the strip's top quarter, amid screams, oaths and pleas from his gambit. Halfway through, the sound stopped, but Gummo kept hacking until the brown mass fell to the ground with a plod and the body toppled down beside it with a flop. 'One less bowel-cleansing vermin in the world.'

He slid out the back door of the shack into a conveniently unlit alley, still cautiously eyeing every corner for possible threats. But it didn't matter now. He knew what he had to do, and he wasn't sure if he'd survive it; he had to set the alarm off on the outer wall of the Orb's fortress in order to free up its minimal entry way. How? Detonate a bomb at the entrance that would make a wider clearway, kill the main source of protection at the gate—the Banana Boys—and hopefully blow the laser system around the Orb. It was almost a gooicide mission.

He moved through the city streets like gravy on a tilted plate, constantly aware of his surroundings. His chemically modified innards slithered around in the hollow of his abdomen. He was created for maximum efficiency and maximum taste experience, his outer gel a totally different flavour to the liquid inside. It made him less solid, lighter on his feet, but meant that he had to rely on weapons against larger enemies.

Rounding a corner, he could see the healthy gloss of the golden gate. He was almost there. It would be over soon, and the Fruits would be getting their comeuppance. But, lost in his own sense of triumph, he didn't notice the mound of earth that concealed the lemon-mine bomb. He grunted in pain as the mound exploded into him, obliterating the lower half of his legs and sending the rest of him into a wall. Amidst his pants of agony, his mind was screaming the danger of being caught. In the half second he had to realise this, his hand reached for a grenade, unhitched the pin and threw it with perfect aim at the glittering gate. The gates clanged apart, and the bananaguards were ripped from their skin, splattered across the street and onto the stone fence. Gummo let the air rush out of his lungs, easing the pressure in his body. It would be a reasonably smooth course from here. The Fruits were too stupid to employ inner guards. His only problem now was the fact that he was missing his legs. His arms were too short to walk on, so the only option was to drag his torso along, agonisingly grating his gel on the gravel. He had no choice.

So he slumped and scratched his way up the street, and through the gate, pausing to ensure the alarm system had been cut off, and that there were no other guards. He continued on into the grounds, heaving with every movement. He was close now. Face down on the ground, the smell of the Enjoyment Orb became stronger by the second, a wafting of laughter and sugar and hyperactivity and rosewater icing. It was all the encouragement he needed. Sliding up the stairs towards the Orb's pedestal, he could taste the saccharine flavour of victory turn to exhilarating ooze in his mouth. This was it.

'You didn't honestly believe that I'd leave the Orb in the care of those lousy Bananas, did you boy?'

Gummo froze. He knew that voice, had known it since it tortured him with celery injections for two whole months. This was the voice that had caused the war, the voice that had caused the loss of love and happiness. A voice reminiscent of the near-salacious malevolence of Alan Rickman. And Gummo knew now that the reason he could smell the Orb so close was that it was in the hands that belonged to that voice.

With great effort, he flipped himself onto his back, and struggled to keep himself from cringing. A safari sunset globe of polished flesh stood before him, one claw stroking the dried greenery on top of the globe, the other tenderly cradling the Enjoyment Orb. Gummo could not see a way out of this.

'Persimmon,' he spat.

The fruit chuckled deeply. 'That's Emperor Persimmon to you, boy.'

Anonymous | UNTITLED

Within the forest grove there lives a
rose that none have seen before.
She grows there on her own,
Upon her thorny throne,
Atop an earthly knoll she rules the
forest grove alone.
Beside a sandy stone she sheds and
grows her petals year by year.
But none may see them fall,
And none may touch their velvet folds,
None must caress those dulcet tones,
for fear they will turn grey.
And let me tell you reader dear,
that none have seen this rose like I.
I glimpsed her one day,
on the sly,
in a sweet repose.
My friend, this rose can sleep and dream!
My friend, this rose can weep and scream!
Believe me,
I have of late seen,
the wonders of this being.
When I am near those rosy limbs,
the earth stands still,
the moon grows dim.
Her fragrant hairs my eyes do sting,
and petals thrash
my heart like wings.
Those branches scratch upon my soul,

her shadow holds me,
all enthralled.
And so the other day I bred a
thought which brought much dread.
This rose I need and cannot live
without her being near.
To own this rose I must attempt,
before the secret's out.
Or live for evermore,
with fear,
and,
loath and doubt.
I hatched my plan with hatchet close and
stumbled through the dark forest.
The moon turned shy and hid my path,
I felt it with my hands and heart.
My rose there stood awaiting,
her beauty radiating,
my heart not abating,
and hands much a-shaking.
I gripped the axe and held my breath, this
heart beat out beyond its chest.
I swung,
and swung,
and swung some more.
But every time,
I could not score.
The rose there still remained,
her silence she retained.
The axe slipped from my hand and tumbled roughly
to the ground.
And so my friend that rose still sits,

beside a stone,
in forest deep.
Her petals still she sheds,
those flowers dark
and red.
But if you don't believe sir, venture
out to see her.
But please remember this, that
hatchet still I keep.
And my hand will not slip,
within that forest deep.

Les Murray | # NUCLEAR FAMILY BEES

Little native-bee hives
clotted all up the trunk
of a big tree by the river.

Not pumped from a common womb
this world of honey flies
is a vertical black suburb

Of glued-on prism cells.
Hunters stopping by
would toe-walk up,

scab off single wax houses
and suck them out, as each
smallholder couple hovered

remonstrating in the air
with their life to rebuild,
new eggs, new sugarbag,

gold skinfuls of water.

Anne Widjaja & Richard Withers |

AFTERWORD

Just in case you were wondering, *ARNA* is not an acronym for an important title that would be indicative of the literary prowess of the Sydney Arts Students Society (SASS). Like many phenomena related to the arts, the title *ARNA* has been capitalised for dramatic, yet utterly meaningless effect. And like the name of this journal, when the title of *ARNA* Editors in Chief was passed on to us, we were determined to make that title meaningful. In this role, we challenged ourselves to realise the full capacity of *ARNA* as a unique and progressive journal that promotes a diversity of style and form across multiple creative/literary mediums. The broad platform of *ARNA* does not simply grant students the opportunity to share their work, it encourages them to do so.

What you have just read, marvelled and subsequently drooled over: every word, reference, typo, impeccably formatted title and artwork in this journal is the culmination of seven months of us repeatedly banging heads with our team of incredibly hardworking editors. Together, we've poured our hearts and minds into trying to make the meaning of *ARNA* really count. Working on behalf of SASS, we have had the luxury of dipping, if not splashing, into the faculty's exceptionally diverse pool of talent to produce a journal that showcases the voice of the University's arts students. Despite having a reliable back-up plan that involved producing a journal comprised entirely of our own works, we were thrilled to have so many gifted and imaginative writers and artists contribute to our humble journal.

The support of the Sydney Arts Student Society, the Arts Faculty and the Union has also left us forever grateful to be part of a university community that grants young writers, artists and editors the opportunity to have their creative works published. We hope that for our contributors, having their work published in *ARNA* is merely the beginning of a fruitful career in the creative arts (please remember us when you're rich and famous, because we will certainly remember you!).

Whether it amounts to a writer's first tentative step toward an ambition of literary success, a designer's first chance to master InDesign or an editor's desire to conquer grammatical errors—the most fulfilling part of having coordinated *ARNA* is that its completion has been celebrated as a shared experience.

We hope you've enjoyed the journey as much as we have.

www.ingramcontent.com/pod-product-compliance
Lightning Source LLC
Chambersburg PA
CBHW071439260626
47170CB00008B/2769